100 BEST

DESSERT

RECIPES

HEARST BOOKS

A Division of Sterling Publishing, Co., Inc.

New York

Published by Hearst Books
A Division of Sterling
Publishing Co., Inc.
387 Park Avenue South,
New York, NY 10016

Good Housekeeping and Hearst Books are
trademarks of Hearst Communications, Inc.

Ellen Levine	Editor in Chief
Susan Westmoreland	Food Director
Susan Deborah Goldsmith	Associate Food Director
Delia Hammock	Nutrition Director
Sharon Franke	Food Appliances Director
Richard Eisenberg	Special Projects Director
Marilu Lopez	Art Director

Supplemental Text by Anne Wright

Book design by Richard Oriolo

The Good Housekeeping Cookbook Seal
guarantees that the recipes in this cookbook meet the strict standards of the Good
Housekeeping Institute, a source of reliable
information and a consumer advocate
since 1900. Every recipe has been triple-
tested for ease, reliability, and great taste.

www.goodhousekeeping.com

**Library of Congress
Cataloging-in-Publication Data**
  Good housekeeping 100 best dessert
  recipes.
    p. cm.
  ISBN 1-58816-323-7
      1. Desserts. I. Title: 100 best
  dessert recipes. II. Goodhousekeeping.
TX773.G614 2004
641.8'6—dc22

                        2003021256

10   9   8   7   6   5   4

Distributed in Canada
by Sterling Publishing
c/o Canadian Manda Group,
165 Dufferin Street,
Toronto, Ontario, Canada M6K 3H6

Distributed in Australia by Capricorn Link
(Australia) Pty. Ltd.
P.O. Box 704, Windsor, NSW 2756
Australia

Manufactured in China

ISBN 1-58816-323-7

Contents

Foreword

Celebrate the sweet things in life—make dessert! Whether you are sharing a meal with friends, commemorating a special event, or just wanting to pack a sweet surprise into a lunchbox, it's dessert that brings on smiles.

I'm always plotting what the best dessert will be, whether we are having a brunch with friends or a fancier dinner party. My husband says I like "earth mother desserts" which translate as fruit-centered or rustic looking finales. The sight of glistening red berries, or any other fruit, sandwiched with cream and shortcake biscuits or nestled under a crumb topping can make me swoon. But so can a triple-layer chocolate cake swirled with vanilla frosting, homemade lemon ice and plum frangipane tart.

There's no doubt that everyone loves desserts. To make things easy and really enticing, we've culled the most requested sweet-treat recipes from our editors and readers for this newest addition to our 100 Best series. Here you'll find sensational finales that will fill out a light meal or lighten a hearty one, and desserts that stand on their own anytime. We also provide recipes for the frostings, toppings, sauces, and decorations that will make these confections a treat for the eyes as well as the taste buds. Of course, like all *Good Housekeeping* cookbooks, the recipes have been triple tested in our kitchens to ensure your success.

So the next time your family turns to you with anticipation and asks, "What's for dessert?", you'll have the answer right at your fingertips.

Susan Westmoreland
FOOD DIRECTOR, *GOOD HOUSEKEEPING*

A Thing or Two About Making Desserts

Dessert-making requires very little in the way of specialized equipment. What follows is information about techniques and tips that will help you achieve perfect desserts.

It All Begins With Measuring

Careful measuring is a cornerstone to successful cooking. For *liquids*, always measure in a glass or plastic measuring cup with a pouring lip. Read the measurement at eye level on a flat surface. For *dry ingredients*, use sets of stainless steel or plastic cups that can be leveled off.

Measuring shortening. Each 1/4-pound stick of butter and margarine measures 1/2 cup or 8 tablespoons. If not using sticks, spoon the shortening in a dry measuring cup or spoon, packing it in firmly; level off with a knife or metal spatula.

Measuring flour. Because flour tends to pack down during storage, stir it in the canister to aerate it before measuring. Lightly spoon the flour into a dry measuring cup; don't pack or shake the cup. Level the excess with a knife or metal spatula. If the recipe calls for 1 cup sifted flour, sift first then measure. If it says 1 cup flour, sifted, measure first then sift.

Measuring sugar. Spoon *granulated or confectioners' sugar* into a dry measuring cup and level off with a knife or metal spatula. When measuring brown sugar, pack it firmly into a dry measuring cup before leveling off.

Measuring syrups. Coat liquid measuring cup or spoon with vegetable oil before adding molasses, honey, corn syrup, etc.; the syrup will slip out easily.

Just Desserts

CREAMY CUSTARD EVERY TIME

Turning out a soft, velvety smooth custard is quite easy if you follow two basic rules: Don't overbeat the eggs and don't turn up the heat.

- Beat the eggs just until the yolks and whites are blended. Overbeating can cause bubbles on the surface of the custard as it bakes.
- Both baked and stove-top custards need gentle heat so they don't separate. For silky top-of-the-stove custards, use low heat and stir constantly to prevent boiling and curdling. Cook baked custards in a water bath (discussion follows) to protect them from the direct heat of the oven.
- A baked custard is done when the center is still jiggly; it will firm as it cools. To check, insert the tip of a knife into the custard about 1 inch from the center; it should come out clean. A stove-top custard is ready when it's thick enough to coat a spoon well. Run your finger across the back of the spoon; it should leave a track.
- Remove baked custard from its water bath immediately. Cool stove-top custard with a piece of plastic wrap directly on the surface so a skin doesn't form.

WATER BATH

Delicately textured desserts are generally baked in a pan of hot water, known as a water bath or *bain-marie*. The water bath helps cook the custard evenly so it doesn't overcook and separate. To set up a water bath, place the filled cooking dish or dishes in a baking or roasting pan large enough to accommodate the dish with a few inches to spare on all sides. Center the pan on a partially pulled-out oven shelf. Fill the pan with hot water to come halfway up the side of the dish, then gently push the shelf back into the oven and bake as directed.

SUCCESSFUL SOUFFLÉS

Warm and fluffy soufflés, with their golden, crusty high-rise tops, are composed of stiffly beaten egg whites, which gives the light texture, and a batter mixture, which provides the flavor.

- Always use a classic soufflé dish or straight-sided custard cups; the straight sides force the expanding soufflé upward.
- Separate eggs right from the refrigerator. Beat the whites until they form firm, glossy peaks but are not dry.
- With a rubber spatula, gently fold in one-third of the whites to lighten the batter, then fold in the remaining whites, half at a time.

- Set the soufflé dish on a rack in center of oven with no racks above it.
- Do not open the oven door to check on the soufflé's progress before three-quarters of the baking time has passed.
- Check for doneness when the soufflé is puffed and golden. Insert a long wooden skewer or sharp knife into the center; it should come out moist. The soufflé should have a soft, slightly underdone texture.
- Bring the soufflé to the table right from the oven; cool air will start to shrink it in 3 to 5 minutes.
- If your soufflé collapses before you get it to the table, just pretend it's supposed to be that way. Drizzle it with sauce or top it with whipped cream and call it a "baked pudding."

THE MYSTIQUE OF MERINGUE

A simple mixture of beaten egg whites and sugar, meringue can be made either soft or hard. The consistency depends on the proportion of sugar to egg whites. Soft meringue has less sugar and is most often used as a topping for pie. Hard meringue has more sugar and is piped into shapes, such as disks or shells, to cradle fruit or cream fillings, and baked to a crisp brittle finish.

- Avoid making meringues on a humid or rainy day because they'll absorb moisture from the air and turn soggy.
- Use clean, dry beaters and a metal or glass, not plastic, bowl.
- Make sure there is not the slightest speck of egg yolk in the whites.
- Beat egg whites until soft peaks form before adding sugar. Add sugar gradually and beat after each addition, until the sugar dissolves completely.
- Gently fold in ingredients such as ground nuts to avoid deflating the whites.
- To give meringue extra crispness and a sparkle, sprinkle with granulated sugar before baking.
- A soft meringue topping is ready when the peaks are brown; a hard meringue will sound hollow when tapped.
- Allow hard meringues to dry completely in the turned-off oven for crisp results. If removed too soon, they'll have a gummy texture.
- Soft meringue pies and tarts are best served within a few hours of baking; hard meringues can be stored up to a week in an airtight container.

A BIT ABOUT CAKES

Cakes are generally classified into two groups: butter and foam.

Butter cakes, such as chocolate, layer, and pound, depend on fat to give them their moist, velvety crumb and rich flavor. The "creaming" stage is crucial; butter and sugar should be beaten together until they take on a pale color and fluffy consistency.

Foam cakes, light, airy chiffon and angel-food cakes, depend on beaten eggs or egg whites for volume and a light texture. Chiffon and sponge cakes contain both egg yolks and whites, and may include vegetable oil, butter, or margarine; angel-food cakes use only egg whites and contain no added fat. Adding cream of tartar to the egg whites before beating gives them better stability; beat until stiff peaks form when beaters are lifted. When combining ingredients, blend the foam gently so it won't deflate. Never grease the pan for an angel or chiffon cake; the batter needs to cling to the sides to rise.

FINGER-LICKIN' FROSTINGS AND FILLINGS

These smooth and creamy additions turn a cake from simple to spectacular.

- Cool cake thoroughly before frosting it. Use a pastry brush to remove any loose crumbs.
- Frost the cake on the serving plate. To keep the plate clean, place strips of waxed paper around the edges of the plate and place the cake on top. After the cake is frosted, carefully pull out the paper strips.
- Spread filling or firm frosting to within 1/2 inch of the edge of the cake layer, very softly filling to within 1 inch of the edge. The weight of the top layer will push it to the edge.
- If the cake is very soft, spread the cake with a thin layer of frosting first, to "set" the crumbs and fill in any imperfections. Allow this coating to dry 5 to 10 minutes, then frost again.
- When filling a decorating bag, stand the narrow end in a measuring cup or glass for ease in handling.
- To keep a cloth decorating bag fresh-smelling, after each use boil it in water with a little baking soda added.
- If you don't have a decorating bag, a sturdy plastic bag makes a good substitute. Fill it with frosting, close with a twist tie, and snip a small hole in one corner.

PERFECT PASTRY FOR PIES AND TARTS

The secret to a successful pie or tart lies in the crust. It should be light and flaky yet stand up to a variety of fillings.

- Start with cold ingredients (chilled butter or margarine, ice-cold water).
- Handle the dough as little as possible to avoid a tough crust.
- When cutting fat into flour, work quickly so the fat remains firm and cold.

- Sprinkle in ice water until the dough is just moistened. Toss quickly and lightly with a fork; do not stir.
- Chill dough for at least 30 minutes to make it easier to roll and help prevent shrinkage.
- Wrap tightly in plastic so edges don't dry out and crack when rolled.
- Roll dough on a lightly floured surface to prevent sticking; sprinkle surface with more flour as needed. Roll dough from center forward and back; rotate dough a quarter turn and repeat rolling and rotating to make an even circle.
- If dough tears, moisten the edges with water and press together.
- Gently ease the dough into a pie plate with your fingertips, pressing out any air pockets. Don't pull the dough to fit, or the crust may shrink during baking.
- For nicely browned piecrusts, use heatproof glass, porcelain, or non-shiny metal pie plates. Shiny metal reflects heat and keeps crusts from browning properly.
- To measure the size of a pie plate, measure across the top of the plate from inside edge to inside edge.

COOKING WITH FRUITS

Choose the best. Select firm, ripe fruit in season. The heavier the fruit feels in your hand, the juicier and better tasting it will be. Smell it: If there's no aroma, there'll be little flavor.

Don't forget to rinse. Wash fruit under gently running water to remove pesticides, waxy coatings, and bacteria. Refrigerate berries and, just before using, rinse in a large bowl of cold water—never in a colander under running water; drain on paper towels.

Sugar to the rescue. The sweetness of individual fruit can vary, so taste the fruit before cooking and adjust the amount of sugar as necessary.

Keep the brown away. Tannins and enzymes in fruits such as apples, peaches, pears, and bananas cause the flesh to discolor when exposed to air. To prevent this, rub the fruit with a cut lemon or briefly place it in a bowl filled with 1 quart of water to which 2 tablespoons of lemon juice have been added.

Cook it gently. If you want the fruit to keep its shape and texture, cook it over low heat just until it's tender.

ICE CREAM AND FROZEN DESSERTS

Before preparing homemade ice cream, read the manufacturer's directions for your particular ice-cream machine.

- For the creamiest texture and maximum yield, make and refrigerate the ice-cream mixture the day before you plan to freeze it (the chilled mixture will also freeze faster).
- Fill the ice-cream machine two-thirds full, so the mixture has room to expand during churning and freezing.
- When making granitas in a pan, the partially frozen mixture is ready for beating when 1 inch around the edge is frozen firm.
- For best flavor, taste the mixture before freezing and add sweetener as necessary. If you're making fruit sorbet, you may need to add some lemon juice to enliven the fruitiness. Allow ice cream to "ripen" in the freezer for at least four hours before serving to fully develop its flavor and texture.

WHIPPED CREAM

Heavy or whipping cream doubles in volume when whipped, so use a bowl that is large enough. Soft peaks (when the cream forms gentle folds) are best for folding into other mixtures to add volume. Stiff peaks (when the cream keeps its shape) can be used as a topping, filling, or frosting. Stiffly whipped cream should stay whipped for several hours before it begins to "weep."

- Cream, bowl, and beaters should be well chilled before beating cream.
- Start with slow speed on mixer to incorporate small air bubbles into it.
- Finish beating at medium speed, until stiff peaks form. Do not overbeat, or cream may break down into butter and whey.
- If you accidentally overbeat the cream and it begins to turn to butter, gently whisk in additional cream 1 tablespoon at a time. Don't beat the cream again or you'll end up with a bowl full of butter.
- If not using whipped cream immediately, cover and refrigerate.

CHOCOLATE

Storing. Chocolate keeps best in a cool, dark place. If stored in too cold conditions, chocolate will "sweat" when brought to room temperature. If storage conditions are too warm, the cocoa butter will start to melt and form a gray "bloom" on the chocolate. This won't affect flavor or color once chocolate is melted.

Melting. All chocolate should be melted over low heat to prevent scorching.

- To speed melting, chop chocolate into small pieces and stir frequently
- When adding liquid to melted chocolate, add at least 2 tablespoons at a time to avoid chocolate clumping and hardening.

Puddings

Raspberry-Banana Trifle

Raspberry-Banana Trifle

This beautiful dessert is easier to make than you think, thanks to store-bought pound cake. To make ahead, fill and slice cake the day before assembling trifle; wrap and refrigerate until ready to use.

PREP I hour plus chilling   **COOK** 5 minutes   **MAKES** 24 servings.

CAKE

I frozen pound cake (I pound), thawed

6 tablespoons seedless red-raspberry jam

CUSTARD

6 large eggs

³/₄ cup sugar

¹/₃ cup cornstarch

4 cups milk

4 tablespoons margarine or butter

2 tablespoons vanilla extract

3 large ripe bananas (I ¹/₂ pounds), sliced

TOPPING

I cup heavy or whipping cream

2 tablespoons sugar

fresh raspberries and fresh mint leaves

I. Prepare cake: With serrated knife, cut crust from pound cake. Place cake on one long side; cut lengthwise into 4 equal slices. With small spatula, spread 2 tablespoons jam on top of 1 cake slice; top with another cake slice. Repeat with remaining jam and cake, ending with cake. Slice jam-layered cake crosswise into ¹/₄-inch-thick slices, keeping slices together, then cut cake lengthwise in half down center. (You should have about 26 jam-layered cake slices cut in half to make 52 half slices.)

2. Prepare custard: In medium bowl, with wire whisk, beat eggs, sugar, and cornstarch; set aside. In 4-quart saucepan, heat milk just to boiling. While constantly beating with whisk, gradually pour about half of hot milk into egg mixture. Pour egg mixture back into milk in saucepan and cook over medium-low heat, whisking constantly, until mixture thickens and begins to bubble around edge of pan (mixture will not boil vigorously). Simmer custard 1 minute, whisking constantly; it must reach a temperature of at least 160°F. Remove saucepan from heat; stir in margarine and vanilla.

3. Assemble trifle: In 4-quart glass trifle dish or deep glass bowl, place 2 rows of cake slices around side of bowl, alternating horizontal and vertical placement of cake slices to make a checkerboard design (see photo at page 11). Place some cake slices in a single layer to cover bottom of bowl; top with one-third of sliced bananas. Spoon one-third of warm custard on top of bananas. Top with half of remaining bananas and half of remaining custard. Top with remaining cake, then bananas and custard. Press plastic wrap onto surface of custard to prevent skin from forming. Refrigerate 6 hours or overnight.

4. Before serving, prepare topping: In small bowl, with mixer at medium speed, beat cream and sugar until stiff peaks form. Remove plastic wrap from trifle; top trifle with whipped cream and garnish with raspberries and mint.

EACH SERVING About 240 calories | **4 g protein** | **28 g carbohydrate** | **12 g total fat (5 g saturated)** | **72 mg cholesterol** | **120 mg sodium.**

Black-and-White Bread Pudding with White-Chocolate Custard Sauce

For chocolate lovers: a sweet bread pudding with two kinds of chocolate. Serve it alone or with sinfully rich White-Chocolate Custard Sauce. (We love the pudding served warm and the sauce cold.)

PREP 40 minutes plus standing **BAKE** 1 hour 15 minutes **MAKES** 16 servings.

1 loaf (16 ounces) sliced firm white bread

9 large eggs

4 cups milk

$^1/_2$ cup sugar

1 tablespoon vanilla extract

$^1/_2$ teaspoon salt

3 ounces white chocolate or white baking bar, grated

3 squares (3 ounces) semisweet chocolate, grated

White-Chocolate Custard Sauce (recipe follows)

1. Preheat oven to 325°F. Grease 13" by 9" baking dish. Place bread slices on large cookie sheet and bake until lightly toasted, about 20 minutes, turning once. Place bread slices in prepared baking dish, overlapping slightly.

2. Meanwhile, in very large bowl, with wire whisk, beat eggs, milk, sugar, vanilla, and salt until well combined. Stir in grated white and semisweet chocolates. Pour milk mixture evenly over bread; let stand 20 minutes, occasionally pressing bread down to absorb milk mixture.

3. Cover baking dish with foil; bake 1 hour. Remove foil and bake until top is golden and knife inserted in center of pudding comes out clean, 15 to 20 minutes longer.

4. Meanwhile, prepare White-Chocolate Custard Sauce.

5. Serve bread pudding warm with custard sauce, or cover and refrigerate to serve cold later.

EACH SERVING WITHOUT SAUCE About 235 calories | 8 g protein | 30 g carbohydrate | 9 g total fat (4 g saturated) | 128 mg cholesterol | 296 mg sodium.

WHITE-CHOCOLATE CUSTARD SAUCE: Finely chop **3 ounces white chocolate or white baking bar**; place in large bowl. Set aside. In small bowl, with wire whisk, beat **4 large egg yolks** and **¼ cup sugar** until well blended. In heavy 2-quart saucepan, heat **1 cup milk** and **¾ cup heavy or whipping cream** over medium-high heat until bubbles form around edge. Beat ⅓ cup hot milk mixture into egg mixture. Slowly pour egg mixture back into milk mixture, stirring rapidly to prevent curdling. Cook over low heat, stirring constantly, until mixture has thickened slightly and coats back of spoon, about 5 minutes. (Mixture should be about 160°F; do not boil, or sauce will curdle.) Pour milk mixture over white chocolate, stirring until chocolate melts and mixture is smooth. Serve custard sauce warm, or refrigerate to serve cold later. Makes about 2½ cups sauce.

EACH TABLESPOON About 41 calories | 1 g protein | 3 g carbohydrate | 3 g total fat (2 g saturated) | 28 mg cholesterol | 7 mg sodium.

Baked Chocolate-Hazelnut Puddings

Bake this rich, soufflélike dessert in individual ramekins. If you like, substitute toasted blanched almonds for the hazelnuts.

PREP 30 minutes plus chilling **BAKE** 25 minutes **MAKES** 8 servings.

4 tablespoons butter or margarine, softened, plus extra for greasing

³/₄ cup hazelnuts, toasted (page 109)

³/₄ cup sugar

7 large eggs, separated

8 squares (8 ounces) semisweet chocolate, melted and cooled

¹/₄ teaspoon salt

³/₄ cup heavy or whipping cream

1 teaspoon vanilla extract

1. Preheat oven to 350°F. Generously butter eight 6-ounce ramekins; set aside.

2. In food processor with knife blade attached, process hazelnuts and ¹/₄ cup sugar until very finely ground.

3. In large bowl, with mixer at medium speed, beat 4 tablespoons butter until smooth. Add ¹/₄ cup sugar; beat until creamy. Add egg yolks, one at a time, beating after each addition. Beat in hazelnut mixture and chocolate until blended.

4. In another large bowl, with mixer at high speed, beat egg whites, salt, and remaining ¹/₄ cup sugar until stiff peaks form when beaters are lifted. Stir one-fourth of beaten whites into chocolate mixture until well combined. Gently fold remaining whites into chocolate mixture. Spoon batter into prepared ramekins. Cover and refrigerate 4 hours or overnight.

5. Preheat oven to 350°F. Place ramekins in large roasting pan (17" by 11 ¹/₂"); place pan in oven. Carefully pour *boiling water* into roasting pan to come halfway up sides of ramekins. Bake until knife inserted in centers comes out with some fudgy batter stuck to it, about 25 minutes. Cool ramekins on wire rack 5 minutes.

6. Meanwhile, in small bowl, with mixer at medium speed, beat cream and vanilla until soft peaks form when beaters are lifted.

7. To serve, scoop out small amount of pudding mixture from top of each dessert; fill with some whipped cream. Replace scooped-out pudding over cream. Serve puddings with remaining whipped cream.

EACH SERVING About 500 calories | 10 g protein | 37 g carbohydrate | 37 g total fat (17 g saturated) | 235 mg cholesterol | 215 mg sodium.

"Log Cabin" Pudding

Peoble Brehm received this recipe from her grade-school teacher in the 1920s. Before she died, Mrs. Brehm made sure that each of her grandchildren knew how to make this family favorite. *Good Housekeeping* friend, Jeff Dibler, passed it on to us.

PREP 40 minutes plus chilling   **MAKES** 16 servings.

2 envelopes unflavored gelatin

$^1/_3$ cup cold water

1 cup maple-flavored syrup

2 cups milk

1 cup heavy or whipping cream

1 cup pecans, toasted and chopped

30 vanilla wafer cookies, crushed

1. In 2-quart saucepan, evenly sprinkle gelatin over water; let stand 1 minute to soften gelatin. Cook over low heat, stirring frequently, until gelatin has completely dissolved (do not boil), 2 to 3 minutes. Remove from heat; stir in maple syrup.

2. Pour milk into medium bowl; with wire whisk, stir in gelatin mixture until blended. Set bowl with gelatin mixture in larger bowl filled with *ice water*. With rubber spatula, stir gelatin mixture until it is very thick, about 15 minutes. Remove bowl from water bath.

3. In large bowl, with mixer at medium speed, beat cream until stiff peaks form when beaters are lifted. Fold gelatin mixture and pecans into whipped cream until evenly blended.

4. Sprinkle half of cookie crumbs over bottom of shallow $2^1/_2$-quart glass or ceramic baking dish. Top with pudding mixture and sprinkle with remaining crumbs. Cover and refrigerate at least 6 hours or overnight.

EACH SERVING About 200 calories | 3 g protein | 21 g carbohydrate | 12 g total fat (5 g saturated) | 29 mg cholesterol | 40 mg sodium.

Vanilla Rice Pudding with Dried Cherries

The starchy nature of short-grain **Arborio** rice gives this pudding its unsurpassed creaminess.

PREP 15 minutes plus cooling and chilling   **COOK** 1 hour 40 minutes
MAKES 12 servings.

¹/₂ **vanilla bean or 1 tablespoon vanilla extract**

6 cups milk

³/₄ **cup sugar**

³/₄ **cup short-grain rice, preferably Arborio**

¹/₂ **cup dried cherries or raisins**

2 tablespoons dark rum (optional)

¹/₄ **teaspoon salt**

¹/₂ **cup heavy or whipping cream**

1. If using vanilla bean, with knife cut lengthwise in half; scrape out seeds and reserve.

2. In heavy 4-quart saucepan, combine milk, sugar, and vanilla bean pieces and seeds; heat to boiling over medium-high heat, stirring occasionally. (If using vanilla extract, stir in with rum in Step 3.) Stir in rice and heat to boiling. Reduce heat; cover and simmer, stirring occasionally, until mixture is very creamy and has thickened slightly, about 1 hour 25 minutes (pudding will firm upon chilling). Discard vanilla bean.

3. Spoon rice pudding into large bowl; stir in dried cherries, rum, if using, and salt. Cool slightly, then cover and refrigerate until well chilled, 6 hours or up to overnight.

4. Up to 2 hours before serving, in small bowl, with mixer at medium speed, beat cream until stiff peaks form. Using rubber spatula, fold half of whipped cream into rice pudding, then fold in remaining cream.

EACH SERVING About 212 calories | 5 g protein | 31 g carbohydrate | 8 g total fat (5 g saturated) | 31 mg cholesterol | 112 mg sodium.

Brownie Pudding Cake

Two desserts for the price of one! The batter separates during baking into a fudgy brownie on top of a silky chocolate pudding.

PREP 20 minutes **BAKE** 30 minutes **MAKES** 8 servings.

2 teaspoons instant-coffee powder (optional)

2 tablespoons plus 1 3/4 cups boiling water

1 cup all-purpose flour

3/4 cup unsweetened cocoa

1/2 cup granulated sugar

2 teaspoons baking powder

1/4 teaspoon salt

1/2 cup milk

4 tablespoons butter or margarine, melted

1 teaspoon vanilla extract

1/2 cup packed brown sugar

whipped cream or vanilla ice cream (optional)

1. Preheat oven to 350°F. In cup, dissolve coffee powder in 2 tablespoons boiling water, if using.

2. In medium bowl, combine flour, 1/2 cup cocoa, granulated sugar, baking powder, and salt. In 2-cup measuring cup, combine milk, melted butter, vanilla, and coffee, if using. With wooden spoon, stir milk mixture into flour mixture until just blended. Pour into ungreased 8-inch square baking dish.

3. In small bowl, thoroughly combine brown sugar and remaining 1/4 cup cocoa; sprinkle evenly over batter. Carefully pour remaining 1 3/4 cups boiling water evenly over mixture in baking dish; do not stir.

4. Bake 30 minutes (batter will separate into cake and pudding layers). Cool in pan on wire rack 10 minutes. Serve hot with whipped cream, if you like.

EACH SERVING About 238 calories | 4 g protein | 43 g carbohydrate | 7 g total fat (5 g saturated) | 18 mg cholesterol | 267 mg sodium.

Lemon Pudding Cake

A tried-and-true dessert that is just plain wonderful served from the baking dish while steaming hot. Try the orange version, too.

PREP 20 minutes **BAKE** 40 minutes **MAKES** 6 servings.

3 lemons

³/₄ cup sugar

¹/₄ cup all-purpose flour

3 large eggs, separated

1 cup milk

4 tablespoons butter or margarine, melted

¹/₈ teaspoon salt

1. Preheat oven to 350°F. Grease 8-inch square baking dish. From lemons, grate 1 tablespoon peel and squeeze ¹/₃ cup juice. In large bowl, combine sugar and flour. With wire whisk, beat in egg yolks, milk, melted butter, and lemon peel and juice.

2. In small bowl, with mixer at high speed, beat egg whites and salt until soft peaks form when beaters are lifted. With rubber spatula, fold one-third of egg whites into lemon mixture; gently fold in remaining egg whites just until blended. Pour batter into prepared baking dish.

3. Place baking dish in medium roasting pan (14" by 10"); place in oven. Carefully pour enough *very hot water* into roasting pan to come halfway up sides of baking dish. Bake until top is golden and set, about 40 minutes (batter will separate into cake and pudding layers). Cool in pan on wire rack 10 minutes. Serve hot.

EACH SERVING About 256 calories I 5 g protein I 32 g carbohydrate I 12 g total fat (7 g saturated) I 133 mg cholesterol I 179 mg sodium.

Orange Pudding Cake

Prepare as directed, but in Step 1, use ¹/₄ cup fresh lemon juice, ¹/₄ cup fresh orange juice, and 2 teaspoons freshly grated orange peel.

Chocolate Soufflés

These always make an impressive dessert. They are irresistible as individual soufflés and spectacular baked as one large soufflé.

PREP 20 minutes plus cooling BAKE 25 minutes MAKES 8 servings.

1 1/4 cups plus 3 tablespoons granulated sugar

1/4 cup all-purpose flour

1 teaspoon instant espresso-coffee powder

1 cup milk

5 squares (5 ounces) unsweetened chocolate, chopped

3 tablespoons butter or margarine, softened

4 large eggs, separated

2 large egg whites

2 teaspoons vanilla extract

1/4 teaspoon salt

confectioners' sugar

1. In 3-quart saucepan, combine 1 1/4 cups granulated sugar, flour, and espresso powder. With wire whisk, gradually stir in milk until blended. Cook over medium heat, stirring constantly, until mixture has thickened and boils; boil, stirring, 1 minute. Remove from heat.

2. Stir in chocolate and butter until melted and smooth. With whisk, beat in egg yolks until well blended; stir in vanilla. Cool to lukewarm.

3. Meanwhile, preheat oven to 350°F. Grease eight 6-ounce custard cups or ramekins or 2-quart soufflé dish; sprinkle lightly with remaining 3 tablespoons granulated sugar.

4. In large bowl, with mixer at high speed, beat the 6 egg whites and salt just until stiff peaks form when beaters are lifted. With rubber spatula, gently fold one-third of beaten egg whites into chocolate mixture; fold back into remaining egg whites just until blended.

5. Spoon mixture into prepared custard cups or soufflé dish. (If using custard cups, place in jelly-roll pan for easier handling.) Bake until soufflés have puffed and centers are glossy, 25 to 30 minutes. Dust with confectioners' sugar. Serve immediately.

EACH SERVING About 356 calories | 7 g protein | 44 g carbohydrate | 19 g total fat (10 g saturated) | 122 mg cholesterol | 178 mg sodium.

Orange Liqueur Soufflé

Perhaps the most popular and elegant of all soufflés. Infuse it with your favorite orange liqueur: Grand Marnier, Curaçao, or Triple Sec.

PREP 20 minutes plus cooling   BAKE 30 minutes   MAKES 8 servings.

4 tablespoons butter or margarine

$1/3$ cup all-purpose flour

$1/8$ teaspoon salt

$1 1/2$ cups milk, warmed

$1/2$ cup plus 2 tablespoons granulated sugar

4 large eggs, separated

2 large egg whites

$1/3$ cup orange-flavored liqueur

1 tablespoon freshly grated orange peel

confectioners' sugar

whipped cream (optional)

1. In heavy 2-quart saucepan, melt butter over low heat. Add flour and salt; cook, stirring, 1 minute. With wire whisk, gradually whisk in warm milk. Cook over medium heat, stirring with wooden spoon, until mixture has thickened and boils. Reduce heat and simmer 1 minute. Remove from heat.

2. With wire whisk, stir $1/2$ cup granulated sugar into milk mixture. Gradually whisk in egg yolks, stirring rapidly to prevent curdling. Cool egg-yolk mixture to lukewarm, stirring occasionally. Stir in orange liqueur and orange peel.

3. Preheat oven to 375°F. Grease 2-quart soufflé dish with butter and evenly sprinkle with remaining 2 tablespoons granulated sugar.

4. In large bowl, with mixer at high speed, beat the 6 egg whites until stiff peaks form when beaters are lifted. With rubber spatula, gently fold one-third of beaten egg whites into egg-yolk mixture; fold back into remaining egg whites just until blended.

5. Spoon mixture into prepared soufflé dish. If desired, to create top-hat effect (center will rise higher than edge), with back of spoon, make 1-inch-deep indentation all around top of soufflé about 1 inch from edge of dish. Bake until soufflé has puffed, is golden brown, and knife inserted 1 inch

from edge comes out clean, 30 to 35 minutes. Dust with confectioners' sugar. Serve immediately. If desired, pass whipped cream to spoon onto each serving.

EACH SERVING About 214 calories | **6 g protein** | **26 g carbohydrate** | 10 g total fat (5 g saturated) | 128 mg cholesterol | 162 mg sodium.

Individual Ginger-Pear Soufflés

Whipping up a soufflé has never been simpler: Just make one of our pureed fruit bases and fold in beaten egg whites. For entertaining, prepare and refrigerate the soufflé mixture in ramekins for up to three hours, then bake just before serving.

PREP 45 minutes **BAKE** 12 minutes **MAKES** 6 servings.

4 cups peeled, cored, and coarsely chopped fully ripe pears (5 to 6 pears)

1 tablespoon fresh lemon juice

2 teaspoons minced, peeled fresh ginger

1 tablespoon margarine or butter, melted

2 tablespoons plus ¼ cup sugar

6 large egg whites

½ teaspoon cream of tartar

1 teaspoon vanilla extract

1. In nonreactive 2-quart saucepan, combine chopped pears, lemon juice, and ginger. Cover and cook over medium-high heat until pears are very tender, about 15 minutes. Remove cover and cook, stirring occasionally, until mixture is almost dry and reduced to about 1 cup, 10 to 15 minutes longer.

2. In blender with center cover removed to allow steam to escape, or food processor with knife blade attached, puree pear mixture until smooth. Transfer to large bowl; cool to room temperature.

3. Meanwhile, preheat oven to 425°F. Brush six 6-ounce custard cups or ramekins with melted margarine and sprinkle with 2 tablespoons sugar.

4. In large bowl, with mixer at high speed, beat egg whites and cream of tartar until soft peaks form when beaters are lifted. Gradually sprinkle in remaining ¼ cup sugar, 1 tablespoon at a time, beating until sugar has dissolved. Add vanilla; continue beating until whites stand in stiff peaks when beaters are lifted. With rubber spatula, fold beaten egg whites, one-third at a time, into pear mixture just until blended.

5. Spoon mixture into prepared custard cups. Place cups in jelly-roll pan for easier handling. Bake until soufflés have puffed and are beginning to brown, 12 to 15 minutes. Serve immediately.

EACH SERVING About 180 calories | 4 g protein | 38 g carbohydrate | 3 g total fat (0 g saturated) | 0 mg cholesterol | 80 mg sodium.

Banana Soufflés

Prepare soufflés as directed, but prepare banana puree instead of pear puree: In blender or in food processor with knife blade attached, puree **3 very ripe, large bananas, 1 tablespoon fresh lemon juice**, and ¼ **teaspoon ground cinnamon** until smooth. (You should have about 1 cup). Fold beaten egg whites into banana puree and bake as directed.

EACH SERVING About 150 calories | 4 g protein | 30 g carbohydrate | 2 g total fat (1 g saturated) | 0 mg cholesterol | 80 mg sodium.

Peach or Apricot Soufflés

Prepare soufflés as directed but prepare peach or apricot puree instead of pear puree: Drain **1 can (1 pound, 13 ounces) peaches in heavy syrup or 2 cans (16 ounces each) apricots in heavy syrup**. In blender or food processor with knife blade attached, puree peaches or apricots until smooth. Transfer to 4-quart saucepan and heat to boiling over medium-high heat. Reduce heat to medium-low and cook, stirring occasionally, until puree is reduced to 1 cup, 15 to 20 minutes. Transfer fruit puree to large bowl; cool to room temperature. Stir in **1 tablespoon fresh lemon juice** and ⅛ **teaspoon almond extract**. Fold beaten egg whites into fruit puree and bake as directed.

EACH SERVING About 155 calories | 4 g protein | 32 g carbohydrate | 2 g total fat (0 g saturated) | 0 mg cholesterol | 85 mg sodium.

Raspberry Soufflé

Here's an impressive fat-free dessert you can make in a snap: Just fold store-bought raspberry fruit spread into beaten egg whites and bake. To do ahead, prepare and refrigerate soufflé mixture in soufflé dish up to three hours, then bake as directed just before serving.

PREP 20 minutes   **BAKE** 15 minutes   **MAKES** 6 servings.

²/₃ cup seedless raspberry spreadable
   fruit (no-sugar-added jam)

1 tablespoon fresh lemon juice

4 large egg whites

¹/₂ teaspoon cream of tartar

2 tablespoons sugar

1 teaspoon vanilla extract

1. Preheat oven to 375°F. In large bowl, with wire whisk, beat raspberry fruit spread and lemon juice until blended; set aside.

2. In small bowl, with mixer at high speed, beat egg whites and cream of tartar until soft peaks form when beaters are lifted. Sprinkle in sugar, beating until sugar has dissolved. Add vanilla; continue beating until whites stand in stiff peaks when beaters are lifted.

3. With rubber spatula, fold one-third of whites into raspberry mixture until well blended, then fold in remaining whites. Spoon soufflé mixture into 1 ¹/₂-quart soufflé dish; gently spread evenly.

4. Bake until puffed and lightly browned, 15 to 18 minutes. Serve immediately.

EACH SERVING About 75 calories | 3 g protein | 16 g carbohydrate | 0 g total fat | 0 mg cholesterol | 35 mg sodium.

Mango Mousse

Sweet, thick cream of coconut is the secret behind this dessert—it tastes of the tropics.

PREP 20 minutes plus chilling   **COOK** 2 minutes   **MAKES** 8 servings.

1 envelope unflavored gelatin	1 can (15 ounces) cream of coconut
¼ cup cold water	½ cup fresh lime juice (about 4 large limes)
2 large ripe mangoes, peeled and coarsely chopped (3 cups)	fresh berries (optional)

1. In 1-quart saucepan, evenly sprinkle gelatin over water; let stand 2 minutes to soften gelatin slightly.

2. Meanwhile, in blender, combine mangoes, cream of coconut, and lime juice; puree until smooth.

3. Cook gelatin over low heat, stirring frequently, until it has completely dissolved, 2 to 3 minutes. Add to mango mixture and process to combine. Pour into 8 custard cups. Cover and refrigerate until well chilled, 4 hours or up to overnight. Serve with berries, if you like.

EACH SERVING About 181 calories | 3 g protein | 18 g carbohydrate | 12 g total fat (11 g saturated) | 0 mg cholesterol | 38 mg sodium.

Cherry-Almond Clafouti

Sweet cherries baked in a custardlike pudding are a classic French country dessert. Serve right out of the oven.

PREP 20 minutes BAKE 40 minutes MAKES 12 servings.

I pound dark sweet cherries, pitted

2 cups half-and-half or light cream

4 large eggs

1/3 cup granulated sugar

2 tablespoons amaretto (almond-flavored liqueur)

2/3 cup all-purpose flour

confectioners' sugar

1. Preheat oven to 350°F. Grease 10" by 1 1/2" round baking dish. Place cherries in baking dish.

2. In medium bowl, with wire whisk, beat half-and-half, eggs, sugar, and amaretto until well mixed. Gradually whisk in flour until smooth. Or, in blender, process half-and-half, eggs, sugar, amaretto, and flour until smooth.

3. Pour egg mixture over cherries in baking dish. Bake until custard has set and knife inserted 1 inch from edge comes out clean (center will still jiggle), 40 to 45 minutes. Serve hot or warm, sprinkled with confectioners' sugar.

EACH SERVING About 161 calories | 4 g protein | 20 g carbohydrate | 7 g total fat (4 g saturated) | 86 mg cholesterol | 38 mg sodium.

Lime Pavlova

In this dessert (which is very low in fat but rich in flavor), a creamy fresh lime filling is spooned into a crisp meringue nest. The meringue can be made several days ahead and stored in an airtight container. Fill up to four hours before serving.

PREP 30 minutes plus cooling and chilling **BAKE** 1 hour 15 minutes
MAKES 10 servings.

3 large egg whites

1/4 teaspoon cream of tartar

1/4 teaspoon salt

1/2 cup sugar

1 teaspoon vanilla extract

4 to 6 limes

1 can (14 ounces) lowfat sweetened condensed milk

1 container (8 ounces) plain lowfat yogurt

1 envelope unflavored gelatin

1/4 cup cold water

5 strawberries, each hulled and cut in half

1. Preheat oven to 275°F. Line cookie sheet with foil. Using 9-inch round cake pan or plate as guide, with toothpick, outline circle on foil.

2. In medium bowl, with mixer at high speed, beat egg whites, cream of tartar, and salt until soft peaks form when beaters are lifted. Sprinkle in sugar, 2 tablespoons at a time, beating until sugar has dissolved. Add vanilla; continue beating until egg whites stand in stiff, glossy peaks when beaters are lifted.

3. Spoon meringue inside circle on cookie sheet. With back of tablespoon, make well in center to form "nest" about 1 1/2 inches high at edge. Bake meringue 1 hour 15 minutes. Turn off oven; leave meringue in oven 1 hour to dry. Cool completely on cookie sheet on wire rack.

4. Meanwhile, prepare filling: From limes, grate 2 teaspoons peel and squeeze 1/2 cup juice. In medium bowl, with wire whisk, beat condensed milk, yogurt, and lime peel and juice until well blended.

5. In 1-quart saucepan, evenly sprinkle gelatin over the cold water; let stand 2 minutes to soften slightly. Cook over medium-low heat, stirring

frequently, until gelatin has completely dissolved. Add gelatin to lime mixture and whisk until blended.

6. Set bowl with lime mixture in larger bowl filled with *ice water*. With rubber spatula, stir mixture occasionally until it begins to thicken, about 20 minutes. Remove bowl from water bath.

7. With metal spatula, carefully loosen and separate meringue shell from foil; place on serving plate. Spoon lime filling into meringue shell; refrigerate until set, about 1 hour. Garnish with strawberries and serve.

EACH SERVING About 234 calories | **7 g protein** | **45 g carbohydrate** |
2 g total fat (2 g saturated) | **8 mg cholesterol** | **147 mg sodium.**

Pumpkin Crème Caramel

When it comes to luscious holiday desserts, this one rivals the ever-popular pumpkin pie for fabulous flavor. It serves twelve—perfect for a family gathering.

PREP 30 minutes plus cooling and chilling   **BAKE** 55 minutes   **MAKES** 12 servings.

1¼ cups sugar

¼ cup water

6 strips (3" by 1" each) orange peel

1 can (12 ounces) evaporated milk

1 cup heavy or whipping cream

1 cup solid-pack pumpkin (not pumpkin-pie mix)

6 large eggs

¼ cup orange-flavored liqueur

1 teaspoon vanilla extract

1 teaspoon ground cinnamon

pinch ground nutmeg

pinch salt

1. In heavy 1-quart saucepan, combine ³/₄ cup sugar, water, and orange peel; heat to boiling over high heat. Cook 10 minutes. Discard orange peel; continue cooking sugar mixture until amber in color, about 3 minutes longer. Pour caramel into 9" by 5" loaf pan, tilting pan to coat bottom completely. (Use pot holders to protect your hands.) Set aside.

2. In heavy 2-quart saucepan, combine evaporated milk, cream, and remaining ¹/₂ cup sugar; heat to boiling over medium-high heat, stirring occasionally, until sugar has dissolved and bubbles form around edge.

3. Meanwhile, preheat oven to 350°F. In large bowl, with wire whisk, mix pumpkin, eggs, orange-flavored liqueur, vanilla, cinnamon, nutmeg, and salt until blended.

4. Gradually whisk hot milk mixture into pumpkin mixture until smooth. Pour custard mixture into caramel-coated loaf pan. Place loaf pan in small roasting pan (13" by 9"); place in oven. Carefully pour enough *very hot water* into roasting pan to come halfway up sides of loaf pan. Bake until knife inserted 1 inch from edge of custard comes out clean (center will jiggle slightly), about 55 minutes.

5. Carefully remove loaf pan from water. Allow crème caramel to cool 1 hour in pan on wire rack; refrigerate overnight. To unmold, run tip of

small knife around edges of custard. Invert onto serving plate, shaking pan gently until custard slips out, allowing caramel syrup to drip onto custard.

EACH SERVING About 243 calories | 6 g protein | 28 g carbohydrate | 12 g total fat (7 g saturated) | 143 mg cholesterol | 85 mg sodium.

Fresh Lemon Gelatin

Tart and cooling, this old-fashioned gelatin dessert has a soft set. If you prefer a sweeter dessert, increase the sugar to two-thirds cup.

PREP 10 minutes plus chilling **COOK** 2 minutes **MAKES** 4 servings.

I envelope unflavored gelatin	**$^2/_3$ cup fresh lemon juice**
I$^1/_4$ cups cold water	**$^1/_2$ cup sugar**

In nonreactive 1-quart saucepan, evenly sprinkle gelatin over $^1/_4$ cup water; let stand 2 minutes to soften slightly. Cook over low heat, stirring frequently, until gelatin has completely dissolved, 2 to 3 minutes. Remove from heat and add lemon juice and sugar, stirring until sugar has dissolved. Stir in remaining 1 cup water. Pour into small bowl; cover and refrigerate 4 hours or up to overnight.

EACH SERVING About 113 calories | 2 g protein | 28 g carbohydrate | 0 g total fat | 0 mg cholesterol | 4 mg sodium.

Crème Brûlée

With its brittle caramelized top, this velvety custard has risen from obscurity to become a megastar of the dessert world.

PREP 20 minutes plus cooling and chilling   **BAKE/BROIL** 38 minutes
MAKES 10 servings.

$^1/_2$ **vanilla bean or 2 teaspoons vanilla extract**

1$^1/_2$ **cups heavy or whipping cream**

1$^1/_2$ **cups half-and-half or light cream**

8 large egg yolks

$^2/_3$ **cup granulated sugar**

$^1/_3$ **to** $^1/_2$ **cup packed brown sugar**

1. Preheat oven to 325°F. If using vanilla bean, with knife, cut lengthwise in half; scrape out seeds and reserve. In heavy 3-quart saucepan, heat cream, half-and-half, and vanilla bean and seeds over medium heat

until bubbles form around edge. If using vanilla extract, stir in after cream mixture in Step 2. Remove from heat. With slotted spoon, remove vanilla bean.

2. Meanwhile, in large bowl, with wire whisk, beat egg yolks and granulated sugar until well blended. Slowly stir in hot cream mixture until well combined. Pour cream mixture into ten 4- to 5-ounce broiler-proof ramekins or shallow 2½-quart casserole.

3. Place ramekins or casserole in large roasting pan (17" by 11 ½"); place pan in oven. Carefully pour enough *very hot water* into pan to come halfway up sides of ramekins or casserole. Bake just until set (mixture will still be slightly soft in center), 35 to 40 minutes. Transfer to wire rack to cool to room temperature. Cover and refrigerate until well chilled, at least 3 hours or up to overnight.

4. Up to 2 hours before serving, preheat broiler. Place brown sugar in small sieve; with spoon, press sugar through sieve to evenly cover tops of chilled custards.

5. Place ramekins in jelly-roll pan for easier handling. With broiler rack at closest position to heat source, broil crème brûlée just until sugar melts, 3 to 4 minutes. Serve, or refrigerate up to 2 hours. The melted brown sugar will form a delicious brittle crust.

EACH SERVING About 307 calories | 4 g protein | 25 g carbohydrate | 21 g total fat (12 g saturated) | 232 mg cholesterol | 38 mg sodium.

Crème Caramel

A masterpiece of French dessert making: individual custards in their own caramel sauce.

PREP 15 minutes plus cooling and chilling   BAKE 50 minutes   MAKES 6 servings.

1/4 plus 1/3 cup sugar

4 large eggs

2 cups milk

1 1/2 teaspoons vanilla extract

1/4 teaspoon salt

1. Preheat oven to 325°F. In heavy 1-quart saucepan, heat 1/4 cup sugar over medium heat, swirling pan occasionally, until sugar has melted and is amber in color. Immediately pour into six 6-ounce custard cups or ramekins.

2. In large bowl, with wire whisk, beat eggs and remaining 1/3 cup sugar until blended. Whisk in milk, vanilla, and salt until well combined; pour mixture through strainer into prepared custard cups.

3. Place custard cups in small baking pan; place on rack in oven. Carefully pour enough *very hot water* into pan to come halfway up sides of cups. Bake just until knife inserted 1 inch from center of custards comes out clean, 50 to 55 minutes. Transfer custard cups to wire rack to cool. Cover and refrigerate until well chilled, 3 hours or up to overnight.

4. To serve, run tip of small knife around edge of custards. Invert cups onto dessert plates, shaking cups gently until custards slip out, allowing caramel syrup to drip onto custards.

EACH SERVING About 177 calories | 7 g protein | 24 g carbohydrate |
6 g total fat (3 g saturated) | 153 mg cholesterol | 177 mg sodium.

Pies & Tarts

Praline Cream-Puff Wreath
recipe on page 68

Cheddar-Crust Vermont Apple Pie

Your family will love this **New England** tradition. The dough can be prepared a day ahead if refrigerated, and up to two weeks ahead if frozen. You can make the entire pie up to a day in advance. Reheat, loosely covered with foil, in preheated 350°F oven for about twenty minutes.

PREP I hour plus cooling BAKE I hour I5 minutes MAKES I0 servings.

2¹/₂ cups all-purpose flour	4 to 6 tablespoons cold water
3 ounces shredded extrasharp Cheddar cheese (about ³/₄ cup)	6 large Cortland apples (about 3¹/₄ pounds)
¹/₂ teaspoon salt	I tablespoon lemon juice
3 tablespoons vegetable shortening	²/₃ cup sugar
¹/₂ cup plus 2 tablespoons margarine or butter	¹/₄ teaspoon ground cinnamon

I. In medium bowl, mix 2¹/₄ cups flour, Cheddar cheese, and salt. With pastry blender or two knives used scissor-fashion, cut in shortening and ¹/₂ cup margarine until mixture resembles coarse crumbs. Sprinkle water, 1 tablespoon at a time, into flour mixture, mixing lightly with a fork after each addition until dough is just moist enough to hold together. Shape dough into 2 balls, one slightly larger than the other. Flatten smaller ball into a disk; wrap with plastic and refrigerate until ready to use.

2. On lightly floured surface, with floured rolling pin, roll larger ball of dough into a round 2 inches larger all around than inverted 9¹/₂-inch deep-dish pie plate. Gently ease dough into pie plate; trim edge, leaving 1-inch overhang. Cover and refrigerate at least 30 minutes.

3. Meanwhile, peel, core, and slice apples into ³/₈-inch-thick slices. Place apple slices in large bowl; toss with lemon juice. In small bowl, mix sugar, cinnamon, and remaining ¹/₄ cup flour. Add sugar mixture to apple slices; toss until evenly coated. Spoon apple mixture into chilled piecrust; dot with remaining 2 tablespoons margarine.

4. Preheat oven to 425°F. Roll remaining dough for top crust into 11-inch round. Cut short slashes in top crust to allow steam to escape during baking. Center round over filling in bottom crust. Trim edge, leaving 1-inch overhang. Fold overhang under; bring up over pie-plate rim and pinch to form high decorative edge.

5. Place pie on foil-lined cookie sheet to catch overflow during baking. Bake until apples are tender when pierced with a knife and pie is bubbly, 1 hour 15 minutes. If necessary, cover pie loosely with foil during last 10 minutes of baking to prevent overbrowning. Cool on wire rack 1 hour to serve warm, or cool completely to serve later.

EACH SERVING About 405 calories | 6 g protein | 56 g carbohydrate |
19 g total fat (5 g saturated) | 9 mg cholesterol | 315 mg sodium.

Chedder-Crust Vermont Apple Pie (top);
Chocolate Pecan Pie (bottom)

Very Blueberry Pie

We like to serve this pie with cinnamon-scented whipped cream. Or, if you prefer, add a pinch of cinnamon or grated lemon peel to the filling. If using wild blueberries, increase the cornstarch to one-third cup; they tend to be juicier than cultivated berries.

PREP 25 minutes plus chilling **BAKE** I hour 20 minutes **MAKES** 10 servings.

Pastry Dough for 2-Crust Pie (page 76)

³/₄ **cup sugar**

¹/₄ **cup cornstarch**

pinch salt

6 cups blueberries (about 3 pints)

I tablespoon fresh lemon juice

2 tablespoons butter or margarine, cut into pieces

1. Prepare Pastry Dough for 2-Crust Pie as directed through chilling.

2. Preheat oven to 425°F.

3. In large bowl, combine sugar, cornstarch, and salt. Add blueberries and lemon juice; toss to combine.

4. Use larger disk of dough to line 9-inch pie plate. Spoon blueberry filling into crust; dot with butter. Roll out remaining disk of dough; cut out ³/₄-inch center circle and 1-inch slits to allow steam to escape during baking. Place over filling and make decorative edge.

5. Place pie on foil-lined cookie sheet to catch any overflow during baking. Bake 20 minutes. Turn oven control to 375°F; bake until filling bubbles in center and crust is golden, about 1 hour longer. If necessary, cover pie loosely with foil during last 20 minutes of baking to prevent overbrowning. Cool on wire rack 1 hour to serve warm, or cool completely to serve later.

EACH SERVING About 374 calories | **4 g protein** | **53 g carbohydrate** | 17 g total fat (8 g saturated) | **31 mg cholesterol** | **253 mg sodium.**

Farm-Stand Cherry Pie

This beautiful pie in a rustic cornmeal crust delights both the eyes and the taste buds.

PREP 45 minutes plus chilling and cooling **BAKE** 45 minutes **MAKES** 6 servings.

1 1/2 cups all-purpose flour

1/3 cup plus 1 tablespoon cornmeal

2/3 cup plus 1 teaspoon sugar

1/2 teaspoon plus 1/8 teaspoon salt

1/2 cup cold margarine or butter (1 stick), cut into pieces

4 to 5 tablespoons cold water

2 tablespoons plus 1 teaspoon cornstarch

1 1/2 pounds dark sweet cherries, pitted

1 large egg white

1. Preheat oven to 425°F. In medium bowl, mix flour, 1/3 cup cornmeal, 1/3 cup sugar, and 1/2 teaspoon salt. With pastry blender or two knives used scissor-fashion, cut in margarine until mixture resembles coarse crumbs. Sprinkle water, 1 tablespoon at a time, into flour mixture, mixing with hands until dough comes together (it will feel dry at first). Shape dough into a ball.

2. Sprinkle large cookie sheet with remaining 1 tablespoon cornmeal. Place dampened towel under cookie sheet to prevent it from slipping. With floured rolling pin, roll dough, on cookie sheet, into a 13-inch round. With long metal spatula, gently loosen round from cookie sheet.

3. In large bowl, combine 1/3 cup sugar and cornstarch. Sprinkle half of sugar mixture over center of dough round, leaving a 2 1/2-inch border all around. Add cherries and any cherry juice to sugar mixture remaining in bowl; toss well. With slotted spoon, spoon cherry mixture over sugared area on dough round (reserve any cherry-juice mixture in bowl). Fold dough up around cherries, leaving a 4-inch opening in center. Pinch dough to seal any cracks.

4. In cup, beat egg white and remaining 1/8 teaspoon salt. Brush egg-white mixture over dough; sprinkle with remaining 1 teaspoon sugar. Pour cherry-juice mixture through opening in top of pie. Refrigerate until well chilled, about 30 minutes.

5. Bake pie until crust is golden brown and cherry mixture is gently bubbling, 45 to 50 minutes. If necessary, cover pie loosely with foil during last 10 minutes of baking to prevent overbrowning.

6. As soon as pie is done, use long metal spatula to loosen it from cookie sheet to prevent sticking. Cool 15 minutes on cookie sheet, then slide onto wire rack to cool completely.

EACH SERVING About 460 calories | 6 g protein | 74 g carbohydrate | 17 g total fat (3 g saturated) | 0 mg cholesterol | 435 mg sodium.

Banana Cream Pie

This rich banana filling is also delicious in a traditional 9-inch piecrust (page 75). Be sure to bake and cool the crust before filling.

PREP 30 minutes plus cooling and chilling **BAKE** 10 minutes **MAKES** 10 servings.

Vanilla Wafer–Crumb Crust
   (page 80)
3/4 cup sugar
1/3 cup cornstarch
1/4 teaspoon salt
3 3/4 cups milk

5 large egg yolks
2 tablespoons butter or margarine,
   cut into pieces
1 3/4 teaspoons vanilla extract
3 ripe medium bananas
3/4 cup heavy or whipping cream

1. Prepare Vanilla Wafer–Crumb Crust as directed. Cool completely.

2. Meanwhile, prepare filling: In 3-quart saucepan, combine sugar, cornstarch, and salt; stir in milk. Cook over medium heat, stirring constantly, until mixture has thickened and boils; boil 1 minute. In small bowl, with wire whisk, lightly beat egg yolks; beat in 1/2 cup hot milk mixture. Slowly pour egg-yolk mixture back into milk, stirring rapidly to prevent curdling. Cook over low heat, stirring constantly, until mixture has thickened, about 2 minutes. Remove from heat. Add butter and 1 1/2 teaspoons vanilla; stir until butter melts. Transfer to medium bowl. Press plastic wrap onto surface to prevent skin from forming. Refrigerate, stirring occasionally, until cool, about 1 hour.

3. Slice 2 bananas crosswise. Spoon half of filling into crust. Arrange sliced bananas on top; spoon remaining filling evenly over bananas. Press plastic wrap onto surface; refrigerate at least 4 hours or up to overnight.

4. To serve, prepare topping: In small bowl, with mixer at medium speed, beat cream and remaining 1/4 teaspoon vanilla until stiff peaks form when beaters are lifted; spread over filling. Slice remaining banana; arrange around edge of pie.

EACH SERVING About 367 calories | 6 g protein | 41 g carbohydrate |
21 g total fat (12 g saturated) | 162 mg cholesterol | 216 mg sodium.

Coconut Cream Pie

Prepare as directed but omit bananas; fold ³/₄ **cup sweetened flaked coconut** into filling before spooning into crust. Refrigerate and top with whipped cream as directed. To serve, sprinkle with ¹/₄ **cup sweetened flaked coconut**, toasted.

Chocolate Cream Pie

Win friends and influence people with this indulgent dessert.

PREP 35 minutes plus cooling and chilling **BAKE** 10 minutes **MAKES** 10 servings.

Chocolate Wafer–Crumb Crust (page 80)

$^3/_4$ cup sugar

$^1/_3$ cup cornstarch

$^1/_2$ teaspoon salt

$3^3/_4$ cups milk

5 large egg yolks

3 squares (3 ounces) unsweetened chocolate, melted

2 tablespoons butter or margarine, cut into pieces

2 teaspoons vanilla extract

Chocolate Curls (page 187; optional)

1 cup heavy or whipping cream

1. Prepare Chocolate Wafer–Crumb Crust as directed. Cool.

2. Meanwhile, in heavy 3-quart saucepan, combine sugar, cornstarch, and salt; with wire whisk, stir in milk until smooth. Cook over medium heat, stirring constantly, until mixture has thickened and boils; boil 1 minute. In small bowl, with wire whisk, lightly beat egg yolks. Beat $^1/_2$ cup hot milk mixture into beaten egg yolks. Slowly pour egg-yolk mixture back into milk mixture, stirring rapidly to prevent curdling. Cook over low heat, stirring constantly, until very thick (mixture should be about 160°F).

3. Remove saucepan from heat and stir in melted chocolate, butter, and vanilla until butter melts and mixture is smooth. Pour hot chocolate filling into cooled crust; press plastic wrap onto surface to prevent skin from forming. Refrigerate until filling is set, about 4 hours.

4. Meanwhile, make Chocolate Curls, if using.

5. To serve, in small bowl, with mixer at medium speed, beat cream until stiff peaks form when beaters are lifted; spoon over chocolate filling. Top with chocolate curls, if desired.

EACH SERVING About 417 calories | 7 g protein | 38 g carbohydrate | 28 g total fat (16 g saturated) | 171 mg cholesterol | 329 mg sodium.

Toasted Coconut Cream Pie

Mary Jane Ogilvie Silvia remembers her mother, Scottish-born Margaret Ogilvie, baking this pie every Thanksgiving in Lancaster, Pennsylvania.

PREP 35 minutes plus chilling **BAKE** 20 minutes **MAKES** 10 servings.

PIECRUST

1 cup all-purpose flour

$1/2$ cup sweetened shredded coconut, toasted

6 tablespoons cold margarine or butter, cut into small pieces

2 tablespoons sugar

1 tablespoon cold water

nonstick cooking spray

FILLING

2 cups milk

1 can ($8^1/2$ ounces) cream of coconut (not coconut milk)

$1/3$ cup cornstarch

$1/4$ teaspoon salt

4 large egg yolks

2 tablespoons margarine or butter

1 teaspoon vanilla extract

TOPPING

1 cup heavy or whipping cream

2 tablespoons sugar

$1/2$ teaspoon vanilla extract

2 tablespoons sweetened shredded coconut, toasted

1. Prepare piecrust: Preheat oven to 375°F. Combine flour, coconut, margarine, sugar, and water in food processor with knife blade attached; process, pulsing on and off, until dough just comes together.

2. Spray 9-inch pie plate with nonstick cooking spray. Press dough evenly onto bottom and up side of pie plate, making a small rim. Bake pie shell until golden, about 20 minutes. If necessary, cover edge with foil during last 10 minutes to prevent overbrowning. Cool on wire rack.

3. While pie shell is cooling, prepare filling: In 3-quart saucepan, with wire whisk, mix milk, cream of coconut, cornstarch, and salt until blended. Cook over medium heat, stirring constantly, until mixture thickens and begins to bubble around side of pan, about 7 minutes; boil 1 minute.

4. In small bowl, with wire whisk or fork, lightly beat egg yolks. Beat small amount of hot milk mixture into beaten egg yolks. Slowly pour egg-yolk mixture back into milk mixture, stirring rapidly to prevent curdling. Cook over low heat, stirring constantly, until very thick (mixture should be about 160°F), about 2 minutes.

5. Remove saucepan from heat; stir in margarine and vanilla until margarine melts and mixture is smooth. Pour hot filling into cooled crust; press plastic wrap onto surface to prevent skin from forming. Refrigerate until filling is cold and set, about 4 hours.

6. To serve, prepare topping: In bowl, with mixer at medium speed, beat cream and sugar until stiff peaks form when beaters are lifted. Beat in vanilla. Spread whipped cream over filling. Sprinkle with coconut.

EACH SERVING About 425 calories | **5 g protein** | **40 g carbohydrate** | **28 g total fat (14 g saturated)** | **124 mg cholesterol** | **235 mg sodium.**

Lemon Meringue Pie

Here is our favorite recipe for this classic citrus masterpiece, crowned with billowing meringue.

PREP 45 minutes plus chilling and cooling **BAKE** 30 minutes **MAKES** 10 servings.

Pastry Dough for 1-Crust Pie (page 75)

4 to 6 lemons

1 1/2 cups sugar

1/3 cup cornstarch

1/4 teaspoon plus pinch salt

1 1/2 cups water

3 large eggs, separated

1 large egg white

2 tablespoons butter or margarine, cut into pieces

1/4 teaspoon cream of tartar

1. Prepare Pastry Dough for 1-Crust Pie as directed through chilling.

2. Preheat oven to 425°F. Use dough to line 9-inch pie plate; make decorative edge. Refrigerate or freeze until firm, 10 to 15 minutes.

3. Line pie shell with foil; fill with pie weights or dry beans. Bake 15 minutes. Remove foil with weights; bake until golden, 5 to 10 minutes longer. If shell puffs up during baking, gently press it down with back of spoon. Cool on wire rack.

4. Meanwhile, from lemons, grate 1 tablespoon peel and squeeze 3/4 cup juice; set aside.

5. In 2-quart saucepan, combine 1 cup sugar, cornstarch, and 1/4 teaspoon salt; stir in water. Cook over medium heat, stirring constantly, until mixture has thickened and boils; boil 1 minute. Remove from heat.

6. In small bowl, with wire whisk, beat egg yolks. Stir in 1/3 cup hot cornstarch mixture until blended; slowly pour egg-yolk mixture back into cornstarch mixture in saucepan, stirring rapidly to prevent curdling. Place saucepan over low heat and cook, stirring constantly, until filling is very thick (mixture should be about 160°F), about 4 minutes. Remove from heat; stir in butter until melted, then gradually stir in lemon peel and juice until blended. Pour into cooled pie shell.

7. Turn oven control to 400°F. In small bowl, with mixer at high speed, beat the 4 egg whites, cream of tartar, and remaining pinch salt until soft peaks form when beaters are lifted. Sprinkle in remaining $1/2$ cup sugar, 2 tablespoons at a time, beating until sugar has completely dissolved and egg whites stand in stiff, glossy peaks when beaters are lifted.

8. Spread meringue over filling to edge of pie shell, sealing meringue to edge and swirling with spoon to make attractive top. Bake until meringue is golden, about 10 minutes. Cool on wire rack away from drafts. Refrigerate at least 3 hours for easier slicing or up to 2 days.

EACH SERVING About 321 calories | 4 g protein | 52 g carbohydrate | 11 g total fat (5 g saturated) | 82 mg cholesterol | 224 mg sodium.

Peach Pie

Don't let the summer go by without making at least one fresh peach pie!

PREP 35 minutes plus chilling   BAKE 1 hour 5 to 20 minutes   MAKES 10 servings.

**Pastry Dough for 2-Crust Pie
   (page 76)**

³/₄ cup sugar

¹/₄ cup cornstarch

pinch salt

**3 pounds ripe peaches (9 large),
   peeled, pitted, and sliced (7 cups)**

1 tablespoon fresh lemon juice

**1 tablespoon butter or margarine,
   cut into pieces**

1. Prepare Pastry Dough for 2-Crust Pie as directed through chilling.

2. Preheat oven to 425°F. In large bowl, combine sugar, cornstarch, and salt. Add peaches and lemon juice; gently toss to combine.

3. Use larger disk of dough to line 9-inch pie plate. Spoon peach filling into crust; dot with butter. Roll out remaining disk of dough; cut out ³/₄-inch center circle and 1-inch slits to allow steam to escape during baking. Place dough over filling and make decorative edge.

4. Place pie on foil-lined cookie sheet to catch any overflow during baking. Bake 20 minutes. Turn oven control to 375°F; bake until filling bubbles in center, 45 to 60 minutes longer. If necessary, cover pie loosely with foil during last 20 minutes of baking to prevent overbrowning. Cool on wire rack 1 hour to serve warm, or cool completely to serve later.

EACH SERVING About 360 calories | 4 g protein | 52 g carbohydrate | 16 g total fat (8 g saturated) | 28 mg cholesterol | 236 mg sodium.

Plum Pie

Prepare pie as directed but substitute **3 pounds tart plums (9 large)**, pitted and sliced, for peaches; use **1 cup sugar**.

Pear Pie

Prepare as directed but substitute **3 pounds ripe pears**, peeled, cored, and sliced, for peaches; add **¹/₈ teaspoon ground nutmeg** to sugar mixture.

Pumpkin Pie with Pecan-Caramel Topping

This pie will vanish quickly—pecans in the crust give it extra appeal.

PREP I hour plus cooling   **BAKE** I hour 30 minutes   **MAKES** 12 servings.

CRUST

$^1/_2$ cup pecans, toasted

2 tablespoons sugar

I $^1/_4$ cups all-purpose flour

$^1/_4$ teaspoon salt

4 tablespoons cold margarine or butter

2 tablespoons vegetable shortening

3 tablespoons ice water

PUMPKIN FILLING

I can (15 ounces) solid-pack pumpkin (not pumpkin-pie mix)

$^3/_4$ cup heavy or whipping cream

$^1/_2$ cup milk

$^1/_2$ cup packed light brown sugar

I $^1/_2$ teaspoons ground cinnamon

$^1/_2$ teaspoon salt

$^1/_4$ teaspoon ground nutmeg

$^1/_4$ teaspoon ground ginger

$^1/_4$ teaspoon ground cloves

3 large eggs

PECAN-CARAMEL TOPPING

I cup packed light brown sugar

$^1/_4$ cup heavy or whipping cream

2 tablespoons light corn syrup

2 tablespoons margarine or butter

I teaspoon distilled white vinegar

I cup pecans, toasted and broken

I teaspoon vanilla extract

1. Prepare crust: In food processor with knife blade attached, process toasted pecans and sugar until finely ground. Add flour and salt to nut mixture and pulse to blend. Add margarine and shortening; pulse just until mixture resembles very coarse crumbs. With processor running, add water, stopping just before dough forms a ball. Shape dough into a disk.

2. Preheat oven to 400°F. Between lightly floured sheets of waxed paper, with rolling pin, roll dough into a round 1$^1/_2$ inches larger in diameter than inverted 9-inch pie plate. Dough will be very tender; refrigerate if too soft to roll. Gently ease dough into pie plate; trim edge, leaving 1-inch overhang. Fold overhang under; bring up over pie-plate rim and pinch to form high decorative edge. With fork, prick bottom and side of pie shell at

1-inch intervals to prevent puffing and shrinking during baking. Refrigerate about 30 minutes.

3. Line pie shell with foil; fill with pie weights or dry beans. Bake 20 minutes. Remove foil with weights; bake until lightly browned, about 10 minutes longer. If shell puffs up during baking, gently press it down with back of spoon. Cool on wire rack at least 15 minutes. Turn oven control to 350°F.

4. Prepare filling: In large bowl, with wire whisk, beat pumpkin, cream, milk, brown sugar, cinnamon, salt, nutmeg, ginger, cloves, and eggs until blended. Pour filling into cooled pie shell. Bake until knife inserted 1 inch from edge of pie comes out clean, 50 to 60 minutes. Cool on wire rack until filling is slightly firm, about 1 hour.

5. Prepare topping: In 2-quart saucepan, heat brown sugar, cream, corn syrup, margarine, and vinegar to boiling over high heat, stirring occasionally. (Do not use smaller pan; mixture bubbles up during cooking.) Reduce heat to low; simmer, uncovered, 5 minutes, stirring frequently. Remove saucepan from heat; stir in pecans and vanilla. (Topping will be very thin when hot but will thicken as it cools.) Pour hot topping over cooled pie. Refrigerate pie at least 4 hours or overnight.

EACH SERVING About 435 calories | 5 g protein | 49 g carbohydrate | 25 g total fat (7 g saturated) | 80 mg cholesterol | 254 mg sodium.

Pecan Pie

This southern classic couldn't be richer or more delicious.

PREP 25 minutes plus cooling and chilling   BAKE 1 hour 5 minutes
MAKES 12 servings.

**Pastry Dough for 1-Crust Pie
    (page 75)**

1³/₄ **cups pecan halves (7 ounces)**

³/₄ **cup dark corn syrup**

¹/₂ **cup packed brown sugar**

**4 tablespoons butter or margarine,
    melted**

1 teaspoon vanilla extract

3 large eggs

1. Prepare Pastry Dough for 1-Crust Pie as directed through chilling.

2. Preheat oven to 425°F. Use dough to line 9-inch pie plate; make decorative edge. Refrigerate or freeze until firm, 10 to 15 minutes.

3. Line pie shell with foil; fill with pie weights or dry beans. Bake 15 minutes. Remove foil with weights; bake until golden, 5 to 10 minutes longer. If shell puffs up during baking, gently press it down with back of spoon. Cool on wire rack. Turn oven control to 350°F.

4. Coarsely chop 1 cup pecans.

5. In large bowl, with wire whisk, mix corn syrup, brown sugar, melted butter, vanilla, and eggs until blended. Stir in chopped pecans and remaining pecan halves.

6. Pour pecan filling into cooled pie shell. Bake until filling is set around edge but center jiggles slightly, 45 to 50 minutes. Cool on wire rack at least 1 hour for easier slicing.

EACH SERVING About 353 calories | 4 g protein | 38 g carbohydrate | 22 g total fat (7 g saturated) | 74 mg cholesterol | 177 mg sodium.

Chocolate Pecan Pie

Prepare as directed but use ³/₄ **cup packed dark brown sugar** and add **2 squares (2 ounces) unsweetened chocolate**, melted, to filling with butter. Pictured on page 41.

Raspberry Tart

The unsurpassed flavor of fresh raspberries is glorified in this tangy tart. It's made in a springform pan to give it a handmade look, but use a tart pan if you prefer.

PREP 20 minutes plus chilling **BAKE** 1 hour 5 minutes **MAKES** 8 servings.

Pastry for 9-Inch Tart (page 78)

²/₃ **cup sugar**

¹/₄ **cup all-purpose flour**

4 cups raspberries (about 4 half-pints)

1 cup heavy or whipping cream, whipped (optional)

1. Prepare Pastry for 9-Inch Tart as directed through chilling.

2. Preheat oven to 425°F. Roll dough into 11-inch round; fold into quarters. Ease dough onto bottom and 1 inch up side of 9-inch springform pan. Refrigerate or freeze until firm, 10 to 15 minutes.

3. Line tart shell with foil; fill with pie weights or dry beans. Bake 15 minutes. Remove foil with weights; bake until golden, 5 to 10 minutes longer. If shell puffs up during baking, gently press it down with back of spoon. Remove from oven. Turn oven control to 375°F.

4. In bowl, combine sugar and flour. Add raspberries and gently toss to combine. Spoon raspberry filling into tart shell. Bake until filling bubbles in center, about 45 minutes.

5. Cool completely in pan on wire rack. When cool, carefully remove side of pan. Serve with whipped cream, if desired.

EACH SERVING WITHOUT CREAM About 260 calories ∣ **3 g protein** ∣ **39 g carbohydrate** ∣ **11 g total fat (6 g saturated)** ∣ **23 mg cholesterol** ∣ **160 mg sodium.**

Apple Tarte Tatin

This classic French dessert is simply a caramelized apple tart. Serve it warm with ice cream or whipped cream if you like.

PREP I hour 10 minutes plus chilling BAKE 25 minutes MAKES 10 servings.

Pastry for 9-Inch Tart (page 78)

6 tablespoons butter or margarine

1 cup sugar

1 tablespoon fresh lemon juice

3³/₄ pounds Golden Delicious apples (9 medium), peeled, cored, and each cut in half

1. Prepare Pastry for 9-Inch Tart as directed but roll into 12-inch round and transfer to cookie sheet. Refrigerate.

2. Preheat oven to 425°F. In heavy 10-inch skillet with oven-safe handle (if skillet is not oven-safe, wrap handle in double layer of foil), combine butter, sugar, and lemon juice; cook over medium-high heat until butter melts and mixture bubbles. Place apples in skillet, overlapping them. Cook 10 minutes, turning apples to cook evenly. Carefully turn apples rounded side down; cook until syrup has thickened and is amber in color, 8 to 12 minutes longer. Remove from heat.

3. Place pastry dough round on top of apples in skillet; fold edge of dough under to form rim around apples. With knife, cut six ¹/₄-inch slits in dough so steam can escape during baking. Bake until crust is golden, about 25 minutes.

4. When tart is done, place large platter on top. Wearing oven mitts to protect your hands, quickly turn skillet upside down to unmold tart. Cool 30 minutes to serve warm, or cool completely to serve later.

EACH SERVING About 342 calories | 2 g protein | 52 g carbohydrate | 16 g total fat (9 g saturated) | 37 mg cholesterol | 198 mg sodium.

Peach Tarte Tatin

Prepare as directed but substitute 3³/₄ pounds firm-ripe peaches (11 medium), peeled, halved, and pitted, for apples. Bake and cool as directed.

Pear Tarte Tatin

Prepare as directed but substitute **3³/4 pounds firm-ripe Bosc pears (about 7)**, peeled, cored, and cut lengthwise in half, for apples. Bake and cool as directed.

Brown-Butter Peach Tart

This beautiful dessert is a nice change from the traditional pie: A thin layer of sliced peaches is baked in a buttery egg filling. Make sure to use real butter; margarine and substitutes don't do justice to the recipe.

PREP 40 minutes plus cooling **BAKE** 1 hour **MAKES** 12 servings.

CRUST

7 tablespoons butter (do not use margarine), melted and cooled to room temperature

⅓ cup sugar

¼ teaspoon vanilla extract

1 cup all-purpose flour

pinch salt

BROWN-BUTTER FILLING

½ cup sugar

2 large eggs

¼ cup all-purpose flour

½ cup butter (1 stick; do not use margarine)

3 medium peaches (about 1 pound), peeled and thinly sliced

1. Prepare crust: Preheat oven to 375°F. In medium bowl, stir melted butter, sugar, and vanilla until combined. Stir in flour and salt until dough just begins to come together. Press dough into 9-inch tart pan with removable bottom. Bake crust until golden brown, about 15 minutes.

2. Meanwhile, prepare filling: In small bowl, with wire whisk, beat sugar and eggs until well mixed. Beat in flour until blended; set aside.

3. In 1-quart saucepan, heat butter over medium heat, stirring occasionally, until it has melted and is a dark, nutty brown color but not burned, about 5 minutes. Whisking constantly, pour hot butter in steady stream into egg mixture; whisk until blended.

4. Arrange peach slices decoratively in warm tart shell; pour in brown-butter mixture. Bake until puffed and golden, about 45 minutes. Cool completely on wire rack. Refrigerate leftovers.

EACH SERVING About 250 calories | 3 g protein | 27 g carbohydrate | 15 g total fat (9 g saturated) | 74 mg cholesterol | 165 mg sodium.

Plum Frangipane Tart

Make this tart with red or black plums—it will be equally good.

PREP 30 minutes plus chilling BAKE 1 hour 20 minutes MAKES 12 servings.

Pastry for 11-Inch Tart (page 79)

1 tube or can (7 to 8 ounces) almond paste, crumbled

4 tablespoons butter or margarine, softened

1/2 cup sugar

1/4 teaspoon salt

2 large eggs

2 teaspoons vanilla extract

1/4 cup all-purpose flour

1 1/4 pounds ripe plums (5 large), pitted and each cut into 6 wedges

1. Prepare Pastry for 11-Inch Tart as directed through chilling.

2. Preheat oven to 425°F. Use dough to line 11-inch tart pan with removable bottom. Refrigerate or freeze until firm, 10 to 15 minutes.

3. Line tart shell with foil; fill with pie weights or dry beans. Bake 15 minutes. Remove foil with weights; bake until golden, 5 to 10 minutes longer. If shell puffs up during baking, gently press it down with back of spoon.

4. Meanwhile, in large bowl, with mixer at low speed, beat almond paste, butter, sugar, and salt until almond paste is crumbly. Increase speed to medium-high and beat, frequently scraping bowl with rubber spatula, until well blended, about 3 minutes. (There may be some tiny lumps.) Add eggs and vanilla; beat until smooth. With wooden spoon, stir in flour.

5. Pour almond-paste mixture into warm tart shell. Arrange plums in concentric circles over filling. Bake until golden, 50 to 60 minutes. Cool in pan on wire rack. When cool, carefully remove side of pan.

EACH SERVING About 342 calories | 6 g protein | 37 g carbohydrate | 20 g total fat (8 g saturated) | 66 mg cholesterol | 274 mg sodium.

Cranberry-Almond Tart

Prepare as directed but omit plums. Bake almond filling until golden, about 20 minutes. Cool in pan on wire rack. In 2-quart saucepan, combine **1 cup cranberries**, **³/₄ cup sugar**, **¹/₃ cup water**, and **¹/₂ teaspoon freshly grated orange peel**; heat to boiling over high heat. Reduce heat; simmer until cranberries pop and mixture has thickened slightly, about 5 minutes. Stir in additional **2 cups cranberries**. Set aside until cool. When cool, carefully remove side of pan; spoon cranberry topping over almond filling.

Jeweled Fruit Galettes

Use a mix of whatever fruit you love—peaches, nectarines, plums, apricots, berries, or cherries—for these free-form individual tarts.

PREP 1 hour plus chilling and cooling **BAKE** about 25 minutes **MAKES** 8 servings.

CRUST

1³/4 cups all-purpose flour

2 tablespoons sugar

¹/4 teaspoon baking powder

¹/2 cup cold butter or margarine
   (1 stick), cut into pieces

¹/3 cup sour cream

1 large egg yolk

2 tablespoons water

FRUIT TOPPING

¹/2 cup sugar

2 tablespoons all-purpose flour

¹/2 teaspoon grated fresh lemon peel

pinch grated nutmeg

1¹/2 pounds mixed fruit, such as
   nectarines, plums, peaches,
   apricots (thinly sliced),
   raspberries, blackberries,
   blueberries, grapes, or cherries
   (stems removed, pitted, and
   each cut in half)

2 tablespoons butter or margarine,
   cut into small pieces

1. Prepare crust: In large bowl, mix flour, sugar, and baking powder. With pastry blender or two knives used scissor-fashion, cut in butter until mixture resembles coarse crumbs. In small bowl, with fork, beat sour cream, egg yolk, and water until blended. Drizzle sour-cream mixture over flour mixture and stir with fork until dough begins to hold together. Gather dough into ball; divide in half and shape each half into a rectangle. Wrap each rectangle separately in plastic and refrigerate 30 minutes or freeze 15 minutes, until firm enough to roll.

2. On floured surface, with floured rolling pin, roll one rectangle into a 19" by 6¹/2" strip. Using bowl or plate as a guide, cut out three 6-inch rounds; reserve trimmings. With wide spatula, transfer rounds to large cookie sheet, leaving room for a fourth round; refrigerate. Repeat with remaining dough and another cookie sheet. Gather trimmings; wrap and freeze 10 minutes. Reroll trimmings into a 12" by 6¹/2" strip; cut out 2 more rounds; place one round on each cookie sheet and refrigerate. (Discard remaining trimmings.)

3. Prepare topping: Preheat oven to 400°F. In small bowl, mix ¹/₄ cup sugar, flour, lemon peel, and nutmeg. Sprinkle about 2 teaspoons of the mixture on each dough round, leaving ³/₄-inch border around edge. Arrange fruit over sugar mixture. Fold uncovered dough edges up onto fruit, pleating edges and pressing them together to keep fruit in place. Sprinkle remaining ¹/₄ cup sugar over fruit and dot with butter.

4. Place cookie sheets on two oven racks and bake until crust is well browned and fruit is tender, 25 to 30 minutes, rotating cookie sheets between upper and lower oven racks halfway through baking. With wide spatula, transfer galettes to wire rack to cool.

EACH SERVING About 365 calories | 5 g protein | 48 g carbohydrate | 18 g total fat (11 g saturated) | 71 mg cholesterol | 175 mg sodium.

Praline Cream-Puff Wreath

Also known as "Paris-Brest" (in honor of the bicycle race between Paris and the city of Brest), this cream-puff dough is baked in the shape of a bicycle wheel. We like to serve it at Christmas, so we call it a wreath (see photo on page 39).

PREP 50 minutes plus chilling and cooling BAKE 55 minutes MAKES 12 servings.

2 cups milk

3 large egg yolks

²/₃ cup granulated sugar

3 tablespoons cornstarch

2 teaspoons vanilla extract

Choux Pastry (page 70)

¹/₄ cup water

¹/₃ cup sliced natural almonds, toasted

1 cup heavy or whipping cream

1 tablespoon confectioners' sugar, plus additional for dusting

1. In 3-quart saucepan, heat milk over medium-high heat until bubbles form around edge. Meanwhile, in medium bowl, with wire whisk, beat egg yolks, ¹/₃ cup granulated sugar, and cornstarch until well blended. Gradually whisk about half of hot milk into egg-yolk mixture. Return milk mixture to saucepan and cook, whisking constantly, until mixture has thickened and boils. Reduce heat to low and cook, stirring, 2 minutes.

2. Remove saucepan from heat; stir in vanilla. Pour pastry cream into medium bowl; press plastic wrap onto surface to prevent skin from forming. Refrigerate until well chilled, 2 hours or up to overnight.

3. Meanwhile, preheat oven to 425°F. Grease and flour large cookie sheet. Using 8-inch cake pan or plate as guide, with toothpick, trace circle in flour on prepared cookie sheet. Prepare Choux Pastry.

4. Spoon dough into pastry bag fitted with ¹/₂-inch plain tip. Using tracing as guide, pipe dough in 1-inch-thick ring just inside circle. Pipe second ring outside of first, making sure dough rings touch. With remaining dough, pipe third ring on top of center seam of first two rings. With moistened finger, gently smooth dough rings where ends meet.

5. Bake wreath 20 minutes. Turn oven control to 375°F and bake until

golden, about 25 minutes longer. Remove wreath from oven; with tip of knife, make several small slits to release steam. Bake 10 minutes longer. Transfer wreath to wire rack and cool completely.

6. While wreath is baking, lightly grease cookie sheet. In 1-quart saucepan, combine remaining $1/3$ cup granulated sugar and water; heat to boiling over medium-high heat, swirling pan occasionally, until sugar has dissolved. Boil mixture, without stirring, until amber in color, 5 to 7 minutes. Remove from heat and stir in almonds. Stir mixture over low heat just until it reliquifies. Immediately pour praline mixture onto prepared cookie sheet; spread with back of spoon to $1/2$-inch thickness. Let praline cool on cookie sheet on wire rack until completely cool, about 10 minutes. Break praline into small pieces. In food processor with knife blade attached, process praline to fine powder. With rubber spatula, gently fold praline into chilled pastry cream.

7. In small bowl, with mixer at medium speed, beat cream and 1 tablespoon confectioners' sugar just until stiff peaks form when beaters are lifted.

8. With long serrated knife, slice cooled wreath horizontally in half; remove and discard moist dough from inside. Spoon or pipe pastry cream into bottom of wreath; top with whipped cream. Replace top of wreath. Refrigerate up to 2 hours if not serving right away. To serve, dust with confectioners' sugar.

EACH SERVING About 326 calories | 7 g protein | 26 g carbohydrate | 22 g total fat (11 g saturated) | 178 mg cholesterol | 177 mg sodium.

Choux Pastry

This light, airy pastry is the basis for many glorious desserts. Use the batter while it is still warm to get the highest puff possible.

PREP 10 minutes COOK 5 minutes.

$^1/_2$ cup butter or margarine
    (1 stick), cut into pieces

1 cup water

$^1/_4$ teaspoon salt

1 cup all-purpose flour

4 large eggs

In 3-quart saucepan, combine butter, water, and salt; heat over medium-high heat until butter melts and mixture boils. Remove from heat. Add flour all at once and, with wooden spoon, vigorously stir until mixture leaves side of pan and forms a ball. Add eggs to flour mixture, one at a time, beating well after each addition, until mixture is smooth and satiny. Shape and bake warm dough as directed.

ONE RECIPE About 1,566 calories | 39 g protein | 98 g carbohydrate |
113 g total fat (64 g saturated) | 1,098 mg cholesterol | 1,763 mg sodium.

Éclairs

Why buy éclairs? Nothing can compare to your first bite of a freshly prepared éclair made right at home.

PREP I hour plus chilling, cooling, and standing   BAKE 40 minutes
MAKES about 30 éclairs.

Vanilla or Chocolate Pastry Cream
   (page 74)

Choux Pastry (ipposite)

3 squares (3 ounces) semisweet
   chocolate, chopped

3 tablespoons heavy or whipping
   cream

1. Prepare Vanilla or Chocolate Pastry Cream; cover and refrigerate until ready to use.

2. Preheat oven to 400°F. Grease and flour large cookie sheet. Prepare Choux Pastry. Spoon dough into large pastry bag fitted with $^{1}/_{2}$-inch plain tip. Pipe dough 1 inch apart on prepared cookie sheet in lengths about $3^{1}/_{2}$ inches long and $^{3}/_{4}$ inch wide, to make about 30 éclairs. With moistened finger, gently smooth tops.

3. Bake until golden, about 40 minutes. Remove éclairs from oven; with tip of knife, make small slit in end of each éclair to release steam. Return éclairs to oven and let stand 10 minutes. Transfer éclairs to wire rack to cool completely.

4. With small knife, make hole in one end of each éclair. Whisk pastry cream until smooth; spoon into clean large pastry bag fitted with $^{1}/_{4}$-inch plain tip. Pipe cream into éclairs.

5. In 6-inch skillet or 1-quart saucepan, combine chocolate and cream; heat over low heat, stirring frequently, until chocolate has melted and mixture is smooth. Remove from heat. Dip top of each éclair into chocolate mixture, smoothing with small spatula if necessary. Let stand on wire racks until chocolate sets.

EACH ÉCLAIR About 116 calories | 3 g protein | 12 g carbohydrate |
6 g total fat (4 g saturated) | 70 mg cholesterol | 70 mg sodium.

Napoleons

This classic French pastry can be tailored to suit your taste. Use frozen or homemade puff pastry and fill with chocolate or vanilla pastry cream. Decorate with vanilla glaze with lines of melted chocolate "feathered" through it, or simply dust generously with confectioners' sugar.

PREP 25 minutes plus chilling and cooling   **BAKE** 25 minutes   **MAKES** 12 servings.

Vanilla or Chocolate Pastry Cream
(page 74)

1 sheet frozen puff pastry (half
17 $1/4$-ounce package), thawed

$1/2$ square ($1/2$ ounce) semisweet
chocolate, chopped

1 cup confectioners' sugar

2 tablespoons water

1. Prepare Vanilla or Chocolate Pastry Cream; cover and refrigerate until ready to use.

2. Preheat oven to 400°F. On lightly floured surface, roll out puff pastry dough to 14" by 12" rectangle. Transfer rectangle to ungreased cookie sheet; with fork, prick all over. Cover dough with the second ungreased cookie sheet.

3. Bake until edges of pastry are golden, 20 to 30 minutes. Remove top cookie sheet; bake until golden all over, about 5 minutes longer. Cool on cookie sheet on wire rack.

4. In heavy 1-quart saucepan, melt chocolate over low heat, stirring frequently, until smooth. With serrated knife, cut puff pastry lengthwise into 3 equal strips. With wire whisk, stir pastry cream until smooth. With narrow metal spatula, spread half of pastry cream over 1 puff pastry strip. Place second strip of pastry on top and spread with remaining pastry cream.

5. Place remaining pastry strip upside down on rack. Place melted chocolate in zip-tight plastic bag with a corner cut. Mix confectioners' sugar and water until smooth; pour over pastry strip. Smooth with metal spatula. Quickly pipe chocolate in lengthwise stripes, $3/4$ inch apart, over glaze. Drag tip of small knife crosswise through chocolate stripes at

$^1/_2$-inch intervals to make feathered design. Let glaze set. Place pastry strip, glaze side up, on top of pastry cream. Refrigerate up to 4 hours. To serve, with serrated knife, cut napoleon crosswise into 1-inch-thick slices.

EACH SERVING About 273 calories | 4 g protein | 38 g carbohydrate | 11 g total fat (3 g saturated) | 77 mg cholesterol | 76 mg sodium.

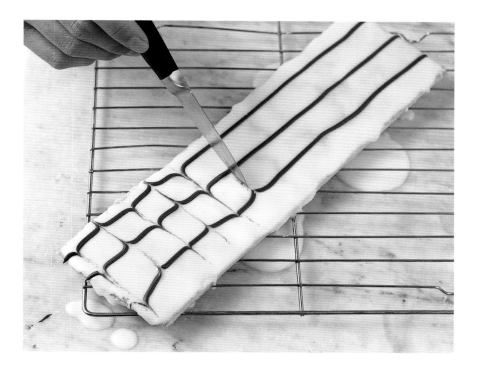

Vanilla Pastry Cream

This versatile cream is used to fill many classic desserts, such as Éclairs (page 71) and Napoleons (72). Be sure to cook the cream for the full two minutes, or it may not set up.

PREP 5 minutes plus chilling   **COOK** 10 minutes   **MAKES** 2 ¾ cups.

2¼ cups milk	¼ cup all-purpose flour
4 large egg yolks	¼ cup cornstarch
⅔ cup sugar	1 tablespoon vanilla extract

1. In 3-quart saucepan, heat 2 cups milk over medium-high heat until bubbles form around edge. Meanwhile, in large bowl, with wire whisk, beat egg yolks, remaining ¼ cup milk, and sugar until combined; whisk in flour and cornstarch until blended. Gradually whisk hot milk into egg-yolk mixture.

2. Return milk mixture to saucepan; cook over medium-high heat, whisking constantly, until mixture has thickened and boils. Reduce heat to low and cook, stirring, 2 minutes.

3. Remove from heat and stir in vanilla. Pour pastry cream into shallow dish. Press plastic wrap onto surface of pastry cream to prevent skin from forming. Refrigerate at least 2 hours or up to overnight.

EACH TABLESPOON About 31 calories | 1 g protein | 5 g carbohydrate | 1 g total fat (0 g saturated) | 21 mg cholesterol | 7 mg sodium.

Chocolate Pastry Cream

Prepare pastry cream as directed but add **3 squares (3 ounces) semisweet chocolate** and **1 square (1 ounce) unsweetened chocolate**, melted, with vanilla. Makes about 3 cups.

EACH TABLESPOON About 44 calories | 1 g protein | 3 g carbohydrate | 3 g total fat (2 g saturated) | 23 mg cholesterol | 37 mg sodium.

Pastry Dough for 1-Crust Pie

Chilling a piecrust before baking helps it retain its shape.

PREP 15 minutes plus chilling   **MAKES** enough dough for one 9-inch crust.

1¼ **cups all-purpose flour**

¼ **teaspoon salt**

4 tablespoons cold butter or margarine, cut into pieces

2 tablespoons vegetable shortening

3 to 5 tablespoons ice water

1. In large bowl, combine flour and salt. With pastry blender or two knives used scissor-fashion, cut in butter and shortening until mixture resembles coarse crumbs.

2. Sprinkle in ice water, 1 tablespoon at a time, mixing lightly with fork after each addition, until dough is just moist enough to hold together.

3. Shape dough into disk; wrap in plastic. Refrigerate 30 minutes or up to overnight. (If chilled overnight, let stand 30 minutes at room temperature before rolling.)

4. On lightly floured surface, with floured rolling pin, roll dough into 12-inch round. Ease dough into pie plate, gently pressing dough against side of plate.

5. Make decorative edge as desired. Refrigerate or freeze until firm, 10 to 15 minutes. Fill and bake as directed in recipe.

EACH ¹⁄₁₀ **PASTRY About 123 calories | 2 g protein | 13 g carbohydrate | 7 g total fat (4 g saturated) | 12 mg cholesterol | 104 mg sodium.**

Pastry Dough for 2-Crust Pie

Every cook should know how to make a from-scratch piecrust. Our perfect recipe gets its flavor from butter and its flakiness from vegetable shortening.

PREP 15 minutes plus chilling **MAKES** enough dough for one 9-inch 2-crust pie.

2¹/₄ cups all-purpose flour

¹/₂ teaspoon salt

¹/₂ cup cold butter or margarine
  (1 stick), cut into pieces

¹/₄ cup vegetable shortening

4 to 6 tablespoons ice water

1. In large bowl, combine flour and salt. With pastry blender or two knives used scissor-fashion, cut in butter and shortening until mixture resembles coarse crumbs.

2. Sprinkle in ice water, 1 tablespoon at a time, mixing lightly with fork after each addition, until dough is just moist enough to hold together.

3. Shape dough into 2 disks, one slightly larger than the other. Wrap each disk in plastic and refrigerate 30 minutes or up to overnight. (If chilled overnight, let stand 30 minutes at room temperature before rolling.)

4. On lightly floured surface, with floured rolling pin, roll larger disk of dough into 12-inch round. Gently roll dough round onto rolling pin and ease into pie plate, pressing dough against side of plate. Trim edge, leaving 1-inch overhang. Reserve trimmings for decorating pie, if you like. Spoon filling into crust.

5. Roll remaining disk of dough into 12-inch round. Cut ³/₄-inch circle out of center and cut 1-inch slits to allow steam to escape during baking; center dough over filling. Fold overhang under; make decorative edge. Bake as directed in recipe.

EACH ¹/₁₀ **PASTRY About 235 calories | 3 g protein | 23 g carbohydrate | 15 g total fat (7 g saturated) | 25 mg cholesterol | 210 mg sodium.**

Food-Processor Pastry Dough

In food processor with knife blade attached, pulse flour and salt to mix. Evenly distribute butter and shortening on top of flour mixture; pulse just until mixture resembles coarse crumbs. With processor running, pour **1/4 cup ice water** through feed tube. Immediately stop motor and pinch dough; it should be just moist enough to hold together. If not, with fork, stir in up to **2 tablespoons additional ice water**. Refrigerate and roll as directed.

Pastry for 9-Inch Tart

This recipe makes enough dough to nicely fit a nine-inch tart pan.

PREP 15 minutes plus chilling **MAKES** enough pastry for one 9-inch tart shell.

I cup all-purpose flour

$^1/_4$ teaspoon salt

6 tablespoons cold butter or margarine, cut into pieces

I tablespoon vegetable shortening

2 to 3 tablespoons ice water

1. In large bowl, combine flour and salt. With pastry blender or two knives used scissor-fashion, cut in butter and shortening until mixture resembles coarse crumbs.

2. Sprinkle in ice water, 1 tablespoon at a time, mixing lightly with fork after each addition, until dough is just moist enough to hold together.

3. Shape dough into disk; wrap in plastic. Refrigerate 30 minutes or up to overnight. (If chilled overnight, let stand 30 minutes at room temperature before rolling.)

4. On lightly floured surface, with floured rolling pin, roll dough into 11-inch round. Ease dough into 9-inch tart pan with removable bottom. Fold overhang in and press dough against side of pan so it extends $^1/_8$ inch above rim. Refrigerate or freeze until firm, 10 to 15 minutes. Fill and bake as directed in recipe.

EACH $^1/_8$ **PASTRY About 151 calories | 2 g protein | 13 g carbohydrate | 10 g total fat (6 g saturated) | 23 mg cholesterol | 160 mg sodium.**

Pastry for 11-Inch Tart

Tart pastry is a bit richer than pie pastry and bakes up crisper.

PREP 15 minutes plus chilling   **MAKES** enough pastry for one 11-inch tart shell.

1 1/2 **cups all-purpose flour**

1/2 **teaspoon salt**

1/2 **cup cold butter or margarine
   (1 stick), cut into pieces**

2 **tablespoons vegetable shortening**

3 to 4 **tablespoons ice water**

1. In large bowl, combine flour and salt. With pastry blender or two knives used scissor-fashion, cut in butter and shortening until mixture resembles coarse crumbs.

2. Sprinkle in ice water, 1 tablespoon at a time, mixing lightly with fork after each addition, until dough is just moist enough to hold together.

3. Shape dough into disk; wrap in plastic. Refrigerate 30 minutes or up to overnight. (If chilled overnight, let stand 30 minutes at room temperature before rolling.)

4. On lightly floured surface, with floured rolling pin, roll dough into 14-inch round. Ease dough into 11-inch tart pan with removable bottom. Fold overhang in and press dough against side of pan so it extends 1/8 inch above rim. Refrigerate or freeze until firm, 10 to 15 minutes. Fill and bake as directed in recipe.

EACH 1/12 **PASTRY About 148 calories | 2 g protein | 13 g carbohydrate |
10 g total fat (5 g saturated) | 21 mg cholesterol | 175 mg sodium.**

Chocolate Truffle Cake

Bake this exceptionally rich dessert a day ahead for best flavor and texture. To serve, dip the knife in hot water before cutting each slice.

PREP 1 hour plus chilling **BAKE** 35 minutes **MAKES** 24 servings.

1 cup butter (2 sticks; do not use margarine)

14 squares (14 ounces) semisweet chocolate

2 squares (2 ounces) unsweetened chocolate

9 large eggs, separated

$^1/_2$ cup granulated sugar

$^1/_4$ teaspoon cream of tartar

confectioners' sugar

1. Preheat oven to 300°F. Remove bottom from 9" by 3" springform pan and cover with foil, wrapping foil around to underside (this will make it easier to remove the cake from the pan). Replace pan bottom. Grease and flour foil bottom and side of pan.

2. In large glass bowl, combine butter and semisweet and unsweetened chocolates. In microwave oven, cook, uncovered, on Medium (50%), $2^1/_2$ minutes; stir. Return chocolate mixture to microwave oven; cook until almost melted, 2 to $2^1/_2$ minutes longer. Stir until smooth. (Or, in heavy 2-quart saucepan, heat butter and semisweet and unsweetened chocolates over low heat, stirring frequently, until melted. Pour chocolate mixture into large bowl.)

3. In small bowl, with mixer at high speed, beat egg yolks and granulated sugar until very thick and lemon-colored, about 5 minutes. Add egg-yolk mixture to chocolate mixture, stirring with rubber spatula until blended.

4. In another large bowl, with clean beaters and with mixer at high speed, beat egg whites and cream of tartar until soft peaks form when beaters are lifted. With rubber spatula or wire whisk, gently fold one-third of beaten egg whites into chocolate mixture. Fold in remaining whites, just until blended.

5. Pour batter into prepared pan; spread evenly. Bake 35 minutes. (Do not overbake; the cake will firm up on standing and chilling.) Cool cake completely in pan on wire rack; refrigerate overnight in pan.

6. To remove cake from pan, run thin knife that has been rinsed under very hot water and dried around edge to loosen cake from side of pan; remove side of pan. Invert onto cake plate; unwrap foil from pan bottom and remove bottom. Carefully peel foil away from cake.

7. Let cake stand 1 hour at room temperature before serving. Just before serving, decorate cake: Sprinkle confectioners' sugar through fine sieve over star stencil for a pretty design. Or dust top of cake with confectioners' sugar.

EACH SERVING WITHOUT CONFECTIONERS' SUGAR About 200 calories | **4 g protein** | **17 g carbohydrate** | **14 g total fat (6 g saturated)** | **100 mg cholesterol** | **110 mg sodium.**

GH Test Kitchen Tip

A store-bought doily makes an easy stencil, or you can create your own design on lightweight cardboard or a manila file folder. Cut the cardboard at least 1 inch larger all around than the cake's surface. Using a mat knife, cut out stars of different sizes or your own design. Place the stencil over the cake and sprinkle with confectioners' sugar (page 81), as we did, or try cocoa, ground nuts, or grated chocolate.

Pumpkin Cheesecake

Pumpkin pie, move over. Here's a deliciously creamy dessert that is bound to be a hit at your next Thanksgiving dinner.

PREP 30 minutes plus cooling and chilling BAKE 1 hour 25 minutes
MAKES 16 servings.

CRUMB CRUST

1 cup graham-cracker crumbs (8 rectangular graham crackers)

3 tablespoons butter or margarine, melted

2 tablespoons sugar

PUMPKIN FILLING

2 packages (8 ounces each) cream cheese, softened

1 ¼ cups sugar

1 can (15 ounces) solid pack pumpkin (not pumpkin pie mix)

¾ cup sour cream

2 tablespoons bourbon or 2 teaspoons vanilla extract

1 teaspoon ground cinnamon

½ teaspoon ground allspice

¼ teaspoon salt

4 large eggs

SOUR-CREAM TOPPING

1 cup sour cream

3 tablespoons sugar

1 teaspoon vanilla extract

1. Preheat oven to 350°F. Tightly wrap outside of 9" by 3" springform pan with heavy-duty foil. In pan, with fork, combine graham-cracker crumbs, melted butter, and sugar; until crumbs are evenly moistened. Press mixture firmly onto bottom of pan. Bake 10 minutes. Cool completely in pan on wire rack.

2. Prepare filling: In large bowl, with mixer at medium speed, beat cream cheese until smooth. Slowly beat in sugar, frequently scraping bowl with rubber spatula, until blended, about 1 minute. Reduce speed to low. Beat in pumpkin, sour cream, bourbon, cinnamon, allspice, and salt. Add eggs, one at time, beating after each addition, just until blended.

3. Scrape pumpkin mixture onto crust and place in large roasting pan. Place pan on oven rack. Carefully pour enough *boiling water* into roasting pan to come 1 inch up side of springform pan. Bake until center of cake barely jiggles, about 1 hour 10 minutes.

4. Prepare topping: In small bowl, with wire whisk, beat sour cream, sugar, and vanilla until smooth. Remove cheesecake from water bath (leave water bath in oven); spread sour-cream mixture evenly over top. Return cake to water bath and bake 5 minutes longer.

5. Remove cheesecake from water bath and transfer to wire rack; remove foil. Run thin knife around edge of cheesecake to prevent cracking during cooling. Cool completely in pan on wire rack. Cover and refrigerate until well chilled, at least 6 hours or up to overnight. Remove side of pan to serve.

EACH SERVING About 307 calories I **5 g protein** I **29 g carbohydrate** I **19 g total fat (11 g saturated)** I **101 mg cholesterol** I **217 mg sodium.**

Banana Cake with Fudge Frosting

Banana and chocolate are always a winning combination. This time, we've baked up three tender cake layers studded with mini chips and stacked them together with a doubly rich frosting.

PREP I hour plus cooling **BAKE** 25 minutes **MAKES** 16 servings.

CAKE

I cup mashed ripe bananas (2 to 3 medium)

1/4 cup buttermilk or sour cream

I teaspoon vanilla extract

2 cups cake flour (not self-rising)

I teaspoon baking powder

1/2 teaspoon baking soda

1/4 teaspoon salt

1/2 cup margarine or butter (I stick), softened

1 1/4 cups sugar

2 large eggs

1/2 cup semisweet-chocolate mini chips (optional)

FUDGE FROSTING

3/4 cup sugar

1/4 cup all-purpose flour

3 tablespoons unsweetened cocoa

I cup milk

I cup margarine or butter (2 sticks), softened

4 squares (4 ounces) semisweet chocolate, melted and cooled

I tablespoon vanilla extract

1. Preheat oven to 350°F. Grease three 8-inch round cake pans. Line bottoms with waxed paper; grease paper. Dust pans with flour.

2. In small bowl, mix bananas, buttermilk, and vanilla. On sheet of waxed paper, combine flour, baking powder, baking soda, and salt.

3. Prepare cake: In large bowl, with mixer at medium speed, beat margarine and sugar, occasionally scraping bowl with rubber spatula, until light and creamy, about 5 minutes. Add eggs, one at a time, beating well after each addition. Reduce speed to low, add flour mixture alternately with banana mixture, beginning and ending with flour mixture. Beat just until blended, occasionally scraping bowl. With wooden spoon, stir in chocolate chips, if using.

4. Divide batter evenly among prepared pans and spread evenly. Stagger pans on two oven racks, placing two on upper rack and one on lower rack, so that pans are not directly above one another. Bake until toothpick inserted in center of each layer comes out clean, 25 to 30 minutes. Cool layers in pans on wire racks 10 minutes. Run thin knife or small metal spatula around edges to loosen layers from sides of pans. Invert onto wire racks. Remove waxed paper; cool completely.

5. Meanwhile, prepare frosting: In 2-quart saucepan, with wire whisk, mix sugar, flour, and cocoa. Slowly whisk in milk until smooth. Cook over medium heat, stirring frequently, until mixture thickens and boils. Reduce heat to low; cook, stirring constantly, 2 minutes. Remove saucepan from heat; cool completely.

6. In large bowl, with mixer at medium speed, beat margarine until creamy. Gradually beat in cooled milk mixture, melted chocolate, and vanilla until evenly blended and a creamy spreading consistency.

7. Place 1 cake layer, rounded side down, on cake plate. With narrow metal spatula, spread $^1/_2$ cup frosting over layer. Top with second cake layer, rounded side up, and spread with another $^1/_2$ cup frosting. Top with remaining cake layer, rounded side up. Spread remaining frosting over top and side of cake. Refrigerate if not serving right away. If cake is very cold, let stand at room temperature 20 minutes before serving.

EACH SERVING About 385 calories | **4 g protein** | **49 g carbohydrate** |
20 g total fat (4 g saturated) | **29 mg cholesterol** | **350 mg sodium.**

Black Forest Cake

The flavors blend best if you assemble this cake a day ahead.

PREP I hour plus chilling   BAKE 25 minutes   MAKES 16 servings.

CHOCOLATE CAKE

2 cups all-purpose flour

I cup unsweetened cocoa

2 teaspoons baking powder

I teaspoon baking soda

$^1/_2$ teaspoon salt

I cup margarine or butter (2 sticks),
softened

2 cups granulated sugar

4 large eggs

I $^1/_3$ cups milk

2 teaspoons vanilla extract

CHERRY FILLING

2 cans (16$^1/_2$ ounces each) pitted
dark sweet cherries (Bing) in
heavy syrup

$^1/_3$ cup kirsch (cherry brandy)

CREAM FILLING

I $^1/_2$ cups heavy or whipping cream

$^1/_2$ cup confectioners' sugar

2 tablespoons kirsch (cherry brandy)

I teaspoon vanilla extract

Chocolate Curls (page 187)

I. Preheat oven to 350°F. Grease three 9-inch round cake pans. Line bottoms with waxed paper; grease paper. Dust pans with flour.

2. Prepare cake: In medium bowl, combine flour, cocoa, baking powder, baking soda, and salt; set aside.

3. In large bowl, with mixer at low speed, beat margarine and granulated sugar until blended. Increase speed to high; beat until creamy, about 2 minutes. Reduce speed to medium-low. Add eggs, one at a time, beating well after each addition. In small bowl, mix milk and vanilla. At low speed, add flour mixture alternately with milk mixture to margarine mixture, beginning and ending with flour mixture. Beat until batter is smooth, occasionally scraping bowl with rubber spatula.

4. Divide batter evenly among prepared cake pans; spread evenly. Stagger pans on two oven racks, placing two on upper rack and one on lower rack, so that pans are not directly above one another. Bake until toothpick inserted in center of each layer comes out almost clean, about 25 minutes. Cool in pans on wire racks 10 minutes. Run thin knife or small metal spatula around edges to loosen cake layers from sides of pans. Invert onto wire racks. Remove and discard waxed paper; cool layers completely.

5. Meanwhile, prepare fillings: Drain cherries well in sieve set over bowl. Reserve $1/2$ cup syrup; stir in kirsch. Set syrup mixture aside. In small bowl, with mixer at medium speed, beat cream, confectioners' sugar, kirsch, and vanilla until stiff peaks form when beaters are lifted.

6. Assemble cake: Prepare Chocolate Curls as directed. Place 1 layer on cake stand or serving plate; brush with one-third syrup mixture. Spread with one-third whipped-cream mixture, then top with half of cherries. Place second layer on top of cherries. Brush with half of remaining syrup mixture, spread with half of remaining cream mixture, and all of remaining cherries. Top with third layer; brush with remaining syrup mixture. Spoon remaining cream mixture onto center of top layer, leaving a border of cake around edge. Pile chocolate curls on top of whipped cream in center of cake. Cover and refrigerate cake overnight.

EACH SERVING About 450 calories | **6 g protein** | **58 g carbohydrate** | **22 g total fat (8 g saturated)** | **87 mg cholesterol** | **380 mg sodium.**

Golden Butter Cake

This classic layer cake is a good candidate for our exquisitely light orange frosting, but it is so moist that it can also be baked in a tube pan, dusted with confectioners' sugar, and enjoyed on its own.

PREP 1 hour plus cooling **BAKE** 23 minutes **MAKES** 16 servings.

3 cups cake flour (not self-rising)

1 tablespoon baking powder

$1/2$ teaspoon salt

1 cup butter or margarine (2 sticks), softened

2 cups sugar

4 large eggs

2 teaspoons vanilla extract

1 cup milk

Silky Orange Butter Frosting (recipe follows) or desired frosting

1. Preheat oven to 350°F. Grease three 8-inch round cake pans. Line bottoms with waxed paper; grease paper. Dust pans with flour. Or grease and flour 9-inch fluted tube pan.

2. In medium bowl, combine flour, baking powder, and salt. In large bowl, with mixer at medium-high speed, beat butter and sugar until light and fluffy, about 5 minutes. Add eggs, one at a time, beating well after each addition. Beat in vanilla. Reduce speed to low; add flour mixture alternately with milk, beginning and ending with flour mixture. Beat just until smooth, scraping bowl with rubber spatula.

3. Divide batter evenly among prepared cake pans; spread evenly. Stagger pans on two racks, placing two on upper rack and one on lower rack so that pans are not directly above one another. Bake until toothpick inserted in center of each layer comes out clean, 23 to 28 minutes for 8-inch layers or 50 to 55 minutes for tube pan. Cool in pans on wire racks 10 minutes. Run thin knife around edges to loosen layers from sides of pans. Or, if using fluted tube pan, run tip of knife around edge of cake to loosen. Invert onto wire racks. Remove waxed paper from layers; cool completely.

4. Meanwhile, prepare Silky Orange Butter Frosting.

5. Place 1 layer, rounded side down, on cake plate. With narrow metal spatula, spread ²/₃ cup frosting over layer. Top with second layer, rounded side up, and spread with ²/₃ cup frosting. Place remaining layer, rounded side up, on top. Spread remaining frosting over side and top of cake.

EACH SERVING WITH SILKY ORANGE BUTTER FROSTING About 491 calories | 5 g protein | 60 g carbohydrate | 26 g total fat (16 g saturated) | 120 mg cholesterol | 432 mg sodium.

EACH SERVING WITHOUT FROSTING About 315 calories | 4 g protein | 43 g carbohydrate | 14 g total fat (8 g saturated) | 86 mg cholesterol | 305 mg sodium.

SILKY ORANGE BUTTER FROSTING: In 2-quart saucepan, thoroughly combine **1 cup sugar** and **¹/₂ cup all-purpose flour**. With wire whisk, gradually stir in **1¹/₃ cups milk** until smooth. Cook over medium-high heat, stirring frequently, until mixture has thickened and boils. Reduce heat to low; cook stirring constantly, 2 minutes. Remove saucepan from heat; cool completely. In medium bowl, with mixer at medium speed, beat **1 cup butter or margarine (2 sticks)**, softened, until light and fluffy. Gradually beat in milk mixture; beat in **1 teaspoon freshly grated orange peel**. Makes about 3¹/₄ cups.

Carrot Cake

Legend has it that **George Washington** enjoyed some carrot tea bread in 1783, and it remains one of America's favorite desserts. We've included the classic cream cheese frosting.

PREP 50 minutes plus cooling **BAKE** 55 minutes **MAKES** 16 servings.

2 1/2 cups all-purpose flour

2 teaspoons baking soda

2 teaspoons ground cinnamon

1 teaspoon baking powder

1 teaspoon salt

1/2 teaspoon ground nutmeg

4 large eggs

1 cup granulated sugar

3/4 cup packed light brown sugar

1 cup vegetable oil

1/4 cup milk

1 tablespoon vanilla extract

3 cups loosely packed shredded carrots (about 6 medium)

1 cup walnuts (4 ounces), chopped

3/4 cup dark seedless raisins

Cream Cheese Frosting (recipe follows)

1. Preheat oven to 350°F. Grease 13" by 9" baking pan. Line bottom with waxed paper; grease paper. Dust pan with flour. Or grease and flour 10-inch Bundt pan.

2. In medium bowl, combine flour, baking soda, cinnamon, baking powder, salt, and nutmeg.

3. In large bowl, with mixer at medium-high speed, beat eggs and granulated and brown sugars, frequently scraping bowl with rubber spatula, until blended, about 2 minutes. Beat in oil, milk, and vanilla. Reduce speed to low; add flour mixture and beat, scraping bowl, until smooth, about 1 minute. Fold in carrots, walnuts, and raisins.

4. Spoon batter into prepared pan; spread evenly. Bake until toothpick inserted in center comes out almost clean, 55 to 60 minutes for 13" by 9" cake or about 1 hour for Bundt cake. Cool in pan on wire rack 10 minutes. Run thin knife around edges to loosen cake from sides of pan. Or, if using Bundt pan, run tip of knife around edges to loosen cake from side and center tube of pan. Invert onto wire rack. Remove waxed paper; cool completely.

5. Meanwhile, prepare Cream Cheese Frosting.

6. Transfer cooled cake to cake plate. With narrow metal spatula, spread frosting over sides and top of cake.

CREAM CHEESE FROSTING: In large bowl, with mixer at low speed, beat **2 packages (3 ounces each) cream cheese**, slightly softened; **6 tablespoons butter or margarine**, softened; **3 cups confectioners' sugar**; and **1¹/₂ teaspoons vanilla extract** just until blended. Increase speed to medium. Beat, frequently scraping bowl with rubber spatula, until smooth and fluffy, about 1 minute. Makes about 2¹/₂ cups.

Deluxe Carrot Cake

Prepare cake as directed but omit milk; fold in **1 can (8 to 8¹/₄ ounces) crushed pineapple in unsweetened juice** with carrots, walnuts, and raisins.

EACH SERVING About 556 calories | 6 g protein | 71 g carbohydrate |
28 g total fat (8 g saturated) | 77 mg cholesterol | 443 mg sodium.

Easy Chocolate Buttermilk Cake

This cake is so delectably moist and chocolaty, it can be baked in a Bundt pan and served without any frosting, but for something special, bake it in layers spread with White-Chocolate Butter Frosting.

PREP 45 minutes plus cooling   **BAKE** 30 minutes   **MAKES** 16 servings.

2¼ cups all-purpose flour	1½ cups buttermilk
1¾ cups sugar	1 cup vegetable oil
¾ cup unsweetened cocoa	3 large eggs
2 teaspoons baking soda	1½ teaspoons vanilla extract
1¼ teaspoons salt	White-Chocolate Butter Frosting (recipe follows) or desired frosting

1. Preheat oven to 350°F. Grease two 9-inch round cake pans or 10-inch Bundt pan. Dust pans with cocoa.

2. In large bowl, combine flour, sugar, cocoa, baking soda, and salt.

3. In medium bowl, with wire whisk, mix buttermilk, oil, eggs, and vanilla until blended. Add buttermilk mixture to flour mixture and whisk until smooth.

4. Divide batter evenly between prepared cake pans or pour into Bundt pan; spread evenly. Bake until toothpick inserted in center comes out clean, about 30 minutes for 9-inch layers or about 40 minutes for Bundt cake. Cool in pans on wire racks 10 minutes. Run thin knife around edges to loosen layers from sides of pan. Or, if using Bundt pan, run tip of knife around edges to loosen cake from side and center tube of pan. Invert onto racks to cool completely.

5. Meanwhile, prepare White-Chocolate Butter Frosting.

6. Place 1 layer, rounded side down, on cake plate. With narrow metal spatula, spread ⅔ cup frosting over layer. Top with second layer, rounded side up. Spread remaining frosting over side and top of cake.

WHITE-CHOCOLATE BUTTER FROSTING: In large bowl, with mixer at low speed, beat **1 cup butter (2 sticks; do not use margarine)**, softened; 2

cups confectioners' sugar; 6 ounces white chocolate, Swiss confectionery bars, or white baking bars, melted and cooled; and 3 tablespoons milk just until combined. Increase speed to high; beat, frequently scraping bowl with rubber spatula until light and fluffy, about 2 minutes. Makes about 3¹/₂ cups.

EACH SERVING About 527 calories | 5 g protein | 61 g carbohydrate | 31 g total fat (12 g saturated) | 72 mg cholesterol | 505 mg sodium.

New England Maple-Walnut Cake

Three moist cake layers are flavored with maple syrup and robed in luscious homemade frosting.

PREP 50 minutes plus cooling **BAKE** 25 minutes **MAKES** 16 servings.

²/₃ cup walnuts

I cup sugar

2¹/₄ cups cake flour (not self-rising)

2 teaspoons baking powder

¹/₂ teaspoon salt

¹/₄ teaspoon baking soda

³/₄ cup maple syrup or maple-flavored syrup

¹/₂ cup milk

¹/₂ teaspoon imitation maple flavor

³/₄ cup margarine or butter (1¹/₂ sticks), softened

3 large eggs

Maple Buttercream (recipe follows)

walnut halves (optional)

1. Preheat oven to 350°F. Grease three 8-inch round cake pans. Line bottoms with waxed paper; grease paper. Dust pans with flour.

2. In food processor with knife blade attached, or in blender at medium speed, blend walnuts and 2 tablespoons sugar until walnuts are finely ground.

3. In medium bowl, combine flour, baking powder, salt, and baking soda. In 2-cup measuring cup, mix maple syrup, milk, and maple flavor until blended.

4. In large bowl, with mixer at low speed, beat margarine and remaining sugar until blended. Increase speed to high; beat until mixture has a sandy appearance, occasionally scraping bowl with rubber spatula, about 2 minutes. At medium-low speed, add eggs, one at a time, beating well after each addition.

5. Reduce speed to low; add flour mixture alternately with maple-syrup mixture, beginning and ending with flour mixture. Beat just until smooth, occasionally scraping bowl with rubber spatula. Fold in ground-walnut mixture.

6. Divide batter evenly among prepared pans and spread evenly. Stagger pans on two oven racks, placing two on upper rack and one on lower rack, so that pans are not directly above one another. Bake until toothpick inserted in center of each layer comes out clean, 25 to 30 minutes. Cool layers in pans on wire racks 10 minutes. Run thin knife or small metal spatula around edges to loosen layers from sides of pans. Invert onto wire racks. Remove wax paper; cool completely.

7. Meanwhile, prepare Maple Buttercream.

8. Place 1 cake layer on cake plate; spread with $^2/_3$ cup buttercream. Repeat layering, ending with a cake layer. Spread remaining buttercream over side and top of cake. Garnish with walnut halves, if you like. Refrigerate cake if not serving right away.

MAPLE BUTTERCREAM: In 2-quart saucepan, with wire whisk, mix $^1/_2$ **cup all-purpose flour** and $^1/_3$ **cup sugar** until blended. Gradually whisk in **1 cup milk** and $^2/_3$ **cup maple syrup or maple-flavored syrup** until smooth. Cook over medium-high heat, stirring often, until mixture thickens and boils. Reduce heat to low and cook, stirring constantly, 2 minutes. Cool completely. In large bowl, with mixer at medium speed, beat **1 cup margarine or butter (2 sticks)**, softened, until creamy. Gradually beat in cooled milk mixture. Beat in $^1/_4$ **teaspoon imitation maple flavor**. Increase speed to medium-high; beat until smooth with an easy spreading consistency.

EACH SERVING About 440 calories | 4 g protein | 52 g carbohydrate | 25 g total fat (5 g saturated) | 43 mg cholesterol | 425 mg sodium.

Peanut Butter Cupcakes

These cupcakes are great for kids' parties. If you prefer, omit the chocolate topping and use your favorite frosting instead.

PREP 10 minutes **BAKE** 18 minutes **MAKES** 18 cupcakes.

1³/₄ cups all-purpose flour

1 tablespoon baking powder

¹/₂ teaspoon salt

¹/₂ cup creamy or chunky peanut butter

¹/₄ cup vegetable shortening

³/₄ cup sugar

2 large eggs

³/₄ teaspoon vanilla extract

1 cup milk

1 bar (4 ounces) semisweet or milk chocolate, cut into 18 pieces

1. Preheat oven to 350°F. Line eighteen 2¹/₂-inch muffin-pan cups with paper baking liners.

2. In medium bowl, combine flour, baking powder, and salt.

3. In large bowl, with mixer at medium speed, beat peanut butter and shortening until combined. Add sugar and beat until light and fluffy, about 3 minutes. Add eggs, one at a time, beating well after each addition. Beat in vanilla. Reduce speed to low; add flour mixture alternately with milk, beginning and ending with flour mixture. Beat just until blended, occasionally scraping bowl with rubber spatula.

4. Divide batter evenly among cups. Bake until toothpick inserted in centers of cupcakes comes out clean, about 18 minutes. Place 1 piece of chocolate on top of each cupcake; return to oven until chocolate melts, about 1 minute. With small metal spatula, spread chocolate over tops of cupcakes. Remove from pans and cool on wire rack.

EACH CUPCAKE About 192 calories | 5 g protein | 23 g carbohydrate | 10 g total fat (3 g saturated) | 26 mg cholesterol | 193 mg sodium.

Spice Layer Cake

This recipe makes a triple layer cake that you'll want to serve again and again. The unusual but easy-to-make brown-butter frosting complements the aromatic spices beautifully.

PREP 50 minutes plus cooling **BAKE** 25 minutes **MAKES** 16 servings.

2²/₃ cups all-purpose flour

2¹/₂ teaspoons baking powder

2 teaspoons ground cinnamon

1 teaspoon ground ginger

¹/₂ teaspoon salt

¹/₂ teaspoon ground nutmeg

¹/₄ teaspoon ground cloves

1 cup butter or margarine (2 sticks), softened

1 cup granulated sugar

1 cup packed dark brown sugar

5 large eggs

1 cup milk

Brown-Butter Frosting (recipe follows) or desired frosting

1. Preheat oven to 350°F. Grease three 8-inch round cake pans. Line bottoms with waxed paper; grease paper. Dust pans with flour.

2. In medium bowl, combine flour, baking powder, cinnamon, ginger, salt, nutmeg, and cloves.

3. In large bowl, with mixer at low speed, beat, butter and granulated and brown sugars until blended. Increase speed to medium; beat, frequently scraping bowl with rubber spatula, until light and fluffy, about 5 minutes. Add eggs, one at a time, beating well after each addition. Reduce speed to low; add flour mixture alternately with milk, beginning and ending with flour mixture. Beat just until blended, scraping bowl with rubber spatula.

4. Divide batter evenly among prepared pans and spread evenly. Stagger pans on two oven racks, placing two on upper rack and one on lower rack so that pans are not directly above one another. Bake until toothpick inserted in center of each layer comes out clean, 25 to 30 minutes. Cool layers in pans on wire racks 10 minutes. Run thin knife around edges to loosen layers from sides of pans. Invert onto wire racks. Remove waxed paper; cool completely.

5. Meanwhile, prepare Brown-Butter Frosting.

6. Place 1 layer, rounded side down, on cake plate. With narrow metal spatula, spread $^1/_2$ cup frosting over layer. Top with second layer, rounded side up, and spread with $^1/_2$ cup frosting. Top with remaining layer, rounded side up. Spread remaining frosting over side and top of cake.

BROWN-BUTTER FROSTING: In small skillet, over medium heat, cook **$^1/_2$ cup butter (1 stick)** until melted and lightly browned; let cool. In large bowl, with mixer at medium-low speed, beat butter; **1 package (16 ounces) confectioners' sugar**; **3 tablespoons milk, half-and-half, or light cream**; and **$1^1/_2$ teaspoons vanilla extract** until smooth and blended. Beat in **additional milk** as needed for easy spreading consistency. Increase speed to medium-high; beat frosting until light and fluffy, about 1 minute. Makes about $2^1/_3$ cups.

EACH SERVING About 490 calories | 5 g protein | 73 g carbohydrate | 20 g total fat (12 g saturated) | 116 mg cholesterol | 360 mg sodium.

Silver White Cake

Made without egg yolks, this cake has a pristine ivory color that can be accented with a variety of frostings. We've chosen one based on a delectable combination of semisweet and unsweetened chocolates that gives the frosting its perfect flavor balance.

PREP 1 hour plus cooling **BAKE** 30 minutes **MAKES** 12 servings.

2 cups cake flour (not self-rising)	$^1/_2$ cup vegetable shortening
2 teaspoons baking powder	1 teaspoon vanilla extract
1 teaspoon salt	$^1/_4$ teaspoon almond extract
4 large egg whites	1 cup milk
1 $^1/_4$ cups sugar	Chocolate Butter Frosting (recipe follows) or desired frosting

1. Preheat oven to 350°F. Grease and flour two 8-inch round cake pans.

2. In medium bowl, combine flour, baking powder, and salt. In medium bowl, with mixer at high speed, beat egg whites until soft peaks form when beaters are lifted. Sprinkle in $^1/_4$ cup sugar, 1 tablespoon at a time, beating until sugar has dissolved and egg whites stand in stiff, glossy peaks when beaters are lifted.

3. In large bowl, with mixer at low speed, beat shortening and remaining 1 cup sugar until blended. Increase speed to medium. Beat in vanilla and almond extracts. Reduce speed to low; add flour mixture alternately with milk, beginning and ending with flour mixture. Beat just until smooth, occasionally scraping bowl with rubber spatula. Gently fold in beaten egg whites, one-third at a time, just until blended.

4. Divide batter between prepared pans; spread evenly. Bake until tooth-pick inserted in center of each layer comes out clean, about 30 minutes. Cool in pans on wire racks 10 minutes. Run thin knife around edges to loosen layers from sides of pans. Invert onto racks to cool completely.

5. Meanwhile, prepare Chocolate Butter Frosting.

6. Place 1 layer, rounded side down, on cake plate. With narrow metal spatula, spread $^2/_3$ cup frosting over layer. Top with second layer, rounded side up. Spread remaining frosting over side and top of cake.

CHOCOLATE BUTTER FROSTING: In large bowl, with mixer at low speed, beat **$^3/_4$ cup butter or margarine ($1^1/_2$ sticks)**, softened, **2 cups confectioners' sugar**, and **1 teaspoon vanilla extract** until almost combined. Add **4 squares (4 ounces)** semisweet chocolate, melted and cooled, and **2 squares (2 ounces)** unsweetened chocolate, melted and cooled. Increase speed to high; beat frosting until light and fluffy, about 1 minute. Makes about $2^1/_2$ cups.

EACH SERVING About 492 calories | 4 g protein | 63 g carbohydrate | 26 g total fat (13 g saturated) | 34 mg cholesterol | 423 mg sodium.

Silky Chocolate Butter Frosting

Chocolate lovers will put this at the top of their list. It's a great all-purpose frosting that enhances a variety of cakes.

PREP 10 minutes plus cooling   **COOK** 8 minutes   **MAKES** 3 cups.

$^3/_4$ **cup sugar**

$^1/_4$ **cup all-purpose flour**

3 tablespoons unsweetened cocoa

1 cup milk

1 cup butter or margarine (2 sticks), softened

4 squares (4 ounces) semisweet chocolate, melted and cooled

1 tablespoon vanilla extract

1. In 2-quart saucepan, combine sugar, flour, and cocoa. With wire whisk, gradually stir in milk until smooth. Cook over medium heat, stirring frequently, until mixture has thickened and boils. Reduce heat to low; cook, stirring constantly, 2 minutes. Remove saucepan from heat; cool completely.

2. In medium bowl, with mixer at medium speed, beat butter until creamy. Gradually beat in milk mixture, melted chocolate, and vanilla.

EACH TABLESPOON About 64 calories | 0 g protein | 6 g carbohydrate | 5 g total fat (3 g saturated) | 11 mg cholesterol | 42 mg sodium.

Angel Food Cake

Angel food cake, beloved for its clean flavor and light texture, has an added attraction: It's fat-free!

PREP 30 minutes **BAKE** 35 minutes **MAKES** 16 servings.

I cup cake flour (not self-rising)

¹/₂ cup confectioners' sugar

1²/₃ cups egg whites (12 to 14 large egg whites)

1¹/₂ teaspoons cream of tartar

¹/₂ teaspoon salt

1¹/₄ cups granulated sugar

2 teaspoons vanilla extract

¹/₂ teaspoon almond extract

1. Preheat oven to 375°F. Sift flour and confectioners' sugar through sieve set over small bowl.

2. In large bowl, with mixer at medium speed, beat egg whites, cream of tartar, and salt until foamy. Increase speed to medium-high; beat until soft peaks form when beaters are lifted. Sprinkle in granulated sugar, 2 tablespoons at a time, beating until sugar has dissolved and egg whites stand in stiff, glossy peaks when beaters are lifted. Beat in vanilla and almond extracts.

3. Transfer egg-white mixture to larger bowl. Sift flour mixture, one-third at a time, over beaten egg whites; fold in with rubber spatula just until flour mixture is no longer visible. Do not overmix.

4. Scrape batter into ungreased 9- to 10-inch tube pan; spread evenly. Bake until the cake springs back when lightly pressed, 35 to 40 minutes. Invert cake in pan onto large metal funnel or bottle; cool completely in pan. Run thin knife around edges to loosen cake from side and center tube of pan. Remove from pan and place on cake plate.

EACH SERVING About 115 calories | **3 g protein** | **25 g carbohydrate** | **0 g total fat** | **0 mg cholesterol** | **114 mg sodium.**

Cappuccino Angel Food Cake

Prepare as directed but add **4 teaspoons instant espresso-coffee powder** and **1/2 teaspoon ground cinnamon** to egg whites before beating; use **1 1/2 teaspoons vanilla extract** and omit almond extract. In cup, mix **1 tablespoon confectioners' sugar** with **1/8 teaspoon ground cinnamon**; sprinkle evenly over cooled cake.

Vanilla Chiffon Cake

If you like, dust this tall, handsome cake with confectioners' sugar and serve some fresh berries on the side. The citrus variation is tart, so if you prefer your desserts on the sweet side, use three-quarters cup orange juice and omit the lemon juice.

PREP 20 minutes **BAKE** I hour 15 minutes **MAKES** 16 servings.

2¼ cups cake flour (not self-rising)	½ cup vegetable oil
1½ cups sugar	5 large egg whites, separated
I tablespoon baking powder	2 large egg whites
I teaspoon salt	I tablespoon vanilla extract
¾ cup cold water	½ teaspoon cream of tartar

1. Preheat oven to 325°F. In large bowl, combine flour, 1 cup sugar, baking powder, and salt. Make a well in center; add cold water, oil, egg yolks, and vanilla to well. With wire whisk, stir until smooth.

2. In separate large bowl, with mixer at high speed, beat the 7 egg whites and cream of tartar until soft peaks form when beaters are lifted. Sprinkle in remaining ½ cup sugar, 2 tablespoons at a time, beating until sugar has dissolved and egg whites stand in stiff, glossy peaks when beaters are lifted. With rubber spatula, fold one-third of beaten egg whites into egg-yolk mixture, then fold in remaining egg whites until blended.

3. Scrape batter into ungreased 9- to 10-inch tube pan; spread evenly. Bake until cake springs back when lightly pressed, about 1 hour 15 minutes. Invert cake in pan onto large metal funnel or bottle; cool completely in pan. Run thin knife around edges to loosen cake from side and center tube of pan. Remove from pan and place on serving plate.

EACH SERVING About 217 calories | 4 g protein | 31 g carbohydrate | 9 g total fat (I g saturated) | 66 mg cholesterol | 264 mg sodium.

Citrus Chiffon Cake

Prepare as directed but substitute **1 tablespoon freshly grated orange peel** and **1 teaspoon freshly grated lemon peel** for vanilla, and substitute **¹/₂ cup fresh orange juice** and **¹/₄ cup fresh lemon juice** for cold water. In small bowl, combine **1 cup confectioners' sugar**, **1 teaspoon freshly grated lemon peel**, **¹/₄ teaspoon vanilla extract**, and about **5 teaspoons orange juice** to make a smooth glaze; spoon over cooled cake.

Chocolate-Hazelnut Cake

Rich dark cocoa and ground toasted hazelnuts turn this buttermilk-based cake into a chocolate lover's dream. All you need on top is a shake of powdered sugar and maybe a dollop of fresh whipped cream.

PREP 30 minutes plus cooling **BAKE** 1 hour 15 minutes **MAKES** 24 servings.

I cup hazelnuts (filberts), toasted and skinned (page 109)

2¹/₂ cups granulated sugar

2¹/₄ cups all-purpose flour

I cup unsweetened cocoa

³/₄ teaspoon salt

¹/₂ teaspoon baking powder

¹/₂ teaspoon baking soda

I cup butter or margarine (2 sticks), softened

4 large eggs

I tablespoon vanilla extract

1¹/₄ cups buttermilk

confectioners' sugar (optional)

whipped cream (optional)

mint leaves and fresh fruit for garnish

1. Preheat oven to 325°F. Grease 10-inch square or round tube pan or 12-cup fluted baking pan (such as a Bundt); dust with cocoa.

2. In food processor with knife blade attached, pulse hazelnuts with ¹/₂ cup granulated sugar until nuts are very finely ground, occasionally stopping processor and scraping side with rubber spatula.

3. Transfer nut mixture to medium bowl; stir in flour, cocoa, salt, baking powder, and baking soda; set aside.

4. In large bowl, with mixer at low speed, beat butter with remaining 2 cups granulated sugar until blended, scraping bowl often with rubber spatula. Increase speed to medium-high; beat until creamy, about 3 minutes, occasionally scraping bowl.

5. Reduce speed to low; add eggs, 1 at a time, beating well after each addition. Beat in vanilla. Alternately add flour mixture and buttermilk, beginning and ending with flour mixture; beat just until smooth.

6. Spoon batter into pan and spread evenly. Bake until toothpick inserted in center of cake comes out clean, about 1 hour and 15 minutes.

7. Cool cake in pan on wire rack 15 minutes. For tube pan, with small metal spatula, loosen cake from side and center tube of pan. Invert cake onto cake plate; immediately invert again (so top side is up) onto wire rack to cool completely. For fluted pan, loosen cake from pan. Invert cake directly onto wire rack to cool completely. Sprinkle with confectioners' sugar and serve with whipped cream if you like. Garnish with mint leaves and fresh fruit.

EACH SERVING About 255 calories | 4 g protein | 33 g carbohydrate | 13 g total fat (6 g saturated) | 58 mg cholesterol | 215 mg sodium.

GH Test Kitchen Tip

Toasting nuts brings out their flavor, and in the case of nuts such as hazelnuts, allows the skins to be removed.

To toast almonds, pecans, walnuts, or hazelnuts, preheat the oven to 350°F. Spread the shelled nuts in a single layer on a cookie sheet. Bake, stirring occasionally, until lightly browned and fragrant, about 10 minutes. Toast hazelnuts until the skins begin to peel away. Let the nuts cool completely before chopping.

To skin hazelnuts, wrap the still-warm toasted nuts in a clean kitchen towel and let stand for about 10 minutes. Using the towel, rub off as much of the skins as possible (all of the skin may not come off).

Lemon–Poppy Seed Pound Cake

This tangy-sweet cake keeps well. Store any leftover poppy seeds in the refrigerator. They turn rancid quickly at room temperature.

PREP 25 minutes plus cooling   **BAKE** 1 hour 20 minutes   **MAKES** 16 servings.

2 cups all-purpose flour

2 tablespoons poppy seeds

$^1/_2$ teaspoon baking powder

$^1/_4$ teaspoon baking soda

$^1/_4$ teaspoon salt

2 large lemons

$^3/_4$ cup butter or margarine (1$^1/_2$ sticks), softened

1$^1/_2$ plus $^1/_3$ cups sugar

4 large eggs

1 teaspoon vanilla extract

$^1/_2$ cup sour cream

1. Preheat oven to 325°F. Grease and flour 9" by 5" metal loaf pan.

2. In medium bowl, combine flour, poppy seeds, baking powder, baking soda, and salt. From lemons, grate 1 tablespoon peel and squeeze 3 tablespoons juice.

3. In large bowl, with mixer at low speed, beat butter and 1$^1/_2$ cups sugar until blended. Increase speed to high; beat until light and fluffy, about 5 minutes. Add eggs, one at a time, beating well after each addition, frequently scraping bowl with rubber spatula. Beat in lemon peel and vanilla. Reduce speed to low; add flour mixture alternately with sour cream, beginning and ending with flour mixture. Beat just until smooth.

4. Spoon batter into prepared pan; spread evenly. Bake until toothpick inserted in center comes out clean, about 1 hour 20 minutes. Cool in pan on wire rack 10 minutes. Run thin knife around edges to loosen cake from sides of pan. Remove from pan; place on rack set over waxed paper.

5. In small bowl, combine lemon juice and remaining $^1/_3$ cup sugar. With pastry brush, brush mixture over top and sides of warm cake. Cool completely.

EACH SERVING About 267 calories | 4 g protein | 36 g carbohydrate | 12 g total fat (7 g saturated) | 80 mg cholesterol | 178 mg sodium.

Vanilla Pound Cake

This delicate, finely textured pound cake is not as sweet as some. It's perfect with an afternoon cup of tea.

PREP 20 minutes   **BAKE** I hour to I hour 10 minutes   **MAKES** 20 servings.

1 1/2 cups butter or margarine (3 sticks), softened

2 1/4 cups granulated sugar

6 large eggs

1 tablespoon vanilla extract

3/4 teaspoon salt

3 cups cake flour (not self-rising)

confectioners' sugar

1. Preheat oven to 325°F. Grease and flour 10-inch Bundt pan.

2. In large bowl, with mixer at low speed, beat butter and granulated sugar just until blended. Increase speed to high; beat, frequently scraping bowl with rubber spatula, until light and fluffy, about 5 minutes. Reduce speed to medium. Add eggs, one at a time, beating well after each addition. Add vanilla and salt. Increase speed to high; beat 3 minutes, scraping bowl. With wire whisk, stir in flour just until smooth.

3. Spoon batter into prepared pan; spread evenly. Bake until toothpick inserted near center comes out clean, 1 hour to 1 hour 10 minutes. Cool in pan on wire rack 10 minutes. Run tip of thin knife around edges to loosen cake from side and center tube of pan. Invert onto wire rack to cool completely. Dust with confectioners' sugar.

EACH SERVING About 299 calories | 3 g protein | 36 g carbohydrate | 16 g total fat (9 g saturated) | 101 mg cholesterol | 247 mg sodium.

Jelly Roll

Jelly rolls are easy to make and look sensational on a decorative platter. Fill with your favorite jam.

PREP 20 minutes plus cooling **BAKE** 10 minutes **MAKES** 10 servings.

5 large eggs, separated	**¹/₂ cup all-purpose flour**
¹/₂ cup granulated sugar	**confectioners' sugar**
1 teaspoon vanilla extract	**²/₃ cup strawberry jam**

1. Preheat oven to 350°F. Grease 15¹/₂" by 10¹/₂" jelly-roll pan. Line with waxed paper; grease paper.

2. In large bowl, with mixer at high speed, beat egg whites until soft peaks form when beaters are lifted. Sprinkle in ¹/₄ cup granulated sugar, 1 tablespoon at a time, beating until egg whites stand in stiff, glossy peaks when beaters are lifted. Do not overbeat.

3. In medium bowl, with mixer at high speed, beat egg yolks, remaining ¹/₄ cup granulated sugar, and vanilla until very thick and lemon colored, 8 to 10 minutes. Reduce speed to low; beat in flour until blended. With rubber spatula, gently fold egg-yolk mixture into beaten egg whites just until blended.

4. Evenly spread batter in prepared pan. Bake until cake springs back when lightly pressed, 10 to 15 minutes.

5. Sift confectioners' sugar onto clean kitchen towel. Run thin knife around edges to loosen cake from sides of pan; invert onto towel. Carefully remove waxed paper. Trim ¹/₄ inch from edges of cake. From a short side, roll up cake with towel. Place rolled cake, seam side down, on wire rack; cool completely.

6. Unroll cooled cake. With narrow metal spatula, spread evenly with jam. Starting from same short side, roll up cake (without towel). Place rolled cake, seam side down, on platter and dust with confectioners' sugar.

EACH SERVING About 163 calories | 4 g protein | 30 g carbohydrate | 3 g total fat (1 g saturated) | 106 mg cholesterol | 40 mg sodium.

Apricot-Pecan Fruitcake

This light fruitcake has a mellow brandy flavor and is studded with chunks of tangy apricots and buttery pecans. You can make it up to one week ahead, but it's best to glaze it the day it's served.

PREP 20 minutes plus cooling **BAKE** 1 hour 10 minutes **MAKES** 24 servings.

2¹/₂ packages (6 ounces each) dried apricot halves (2¹/₂ cups), cut into ¹/₂-inch pieces

2 cups pecans (8 ounces), coarsely chopped, plus ²/₃ cup pecan halves

1 tablespoon plus 2 cups all-purpose flour

2 teaspoons baking powder

1 teaspoon salt

1 cup butter or margarine (2 sticks), softened

1¹/₄ cups sugar

5 large eggs

¹/₂ cup brandy

1 tablespoon vanilla extract

¹/₃ cup apricot preserves

1. Preheat oven to 325°F. Grease 9- to 10-inch tube pan.

2. In medium bowl, toss apricots and coarsely chopped pecans with 1 tablespoon flour. In medium bowl, combine remaining 2 cups flour, baking powder, and salt.

3. In large bowl, with mixer at low speed, beat butter and sugar until blended. Increase speed to high; beat, occasionally scraping bowl with rubber spatula, until light and fluffy, about 5 minutes. Reduce speed to low. Add eggs, brandy, vanilla, and flour mixture; beat, scraping bowl, until well blended. Stir in apricot mixture.

4. Spoon batter into prepared pan; spread evenly. Arrange pecan halves on top of batter in two concentric circles. Bake until toothpick inserted in center comes out clean, 1 hour 10 to 20 minutes. Cool in pan on wire rack 10 minutes. Run thin knife around edges to loosen cake from side and center tube of pan; lift tube to separate cake from pan side. Slide knife under cake to separate it from bottom of pan. Invert cake onto wire rack and remove center tube. Turn cake, right side up, onto rack to cool completely.

5. In 1-quart saucepan, heat apricot preserves over medium-high heat, stirring constantly, until melted and bubbling. Strain through sieve set over small bowl. With pastry brush, brush cooled cake with preserves. Or wrap cake and refrigerate up to 1 week, then brush with melted preserves before serving.

EACH SERVING About 300 calories | 4 g protein | 35 g carbohydrate | 17 g total fat (6 g saturated) | 65 mg cholesterol | 233 mg sodium.

Cranberry-Raisin Fruitcake

Prepare as directed but substitute **2 cups walnuts (8 ounces)**, toasted and coarsely chopped, plus **²/₃ cup walnut halves** for pecans and **1¹/₂ cups golden raisins** plus **1 cup dried cranberries** for apricots.

Sour-Cream Pear Coffee Cake

We used **Boscs**, the ultimate baking pears, for delicious results. Serve this for breakfast or teatime.

PREP 25 minutes plus cooling **BAKE** 40 minutes **MAKES** 16 servings.

STREUSEL

$^2/_3$ cup packed light brown sugar

$^1/_2$ cup all-purpose flour

1 teaspoon ground cinnamon

4 tablespoons margarine or butter, softened

$^2/_3$ cup walnuts, toasted (page 109) and chopped

CAKE

$2^1/_2$ cups all-purpose flour

$1^1/_2$ teaspoons baking powder

$^1/_2$ teaspoon baking soda

$^1/_2$ teaspoon salt

$1^1/_4$ cups sugar

6 tablespoons margarine or butter, softened

2 large eggs

$1^1/_2$ teaspoons vanilla extract

$1^1/_3$ cups sour cream

3 firm but ripe Bosc pears (about $1^1/_4$ pounds), peeled, cored, and cut into 1-inch pieces

1. Preheat oven to 350°F. Grease 13" by 9" metal baking pan; dust with flour.

2. Prepare streusel: In medium bowl, with fork, mix brown sugar, flour, and cinnamon until well blended. With fingertips, work in margarine or butter until evenly distributed. Add walnuts and toss to mix; set aside.

3. Prepare cake: In separate medium bowl, combine flour, baking powder, baking soda, and salt; set aside.

4. In large bowl, with mixer at low speed, beat sugar with margarine until blended, scraping bowl often with rubber spatula. Increase speed to high; beat until creamy, about 2 minutes, occasionally scraping bowl. Reduce speed to low; add eggs, 1 at a time, beating well after each addition. Beat in vanilla.

5. With mixer at low speed, alternately add flour mixture and sour cream, beginning and ending with flour mixture, until batter is smooth, occasionally scraping bowl. With rubber spatula, fold in pears.

6. Spoon batter into pan; spread evenly. Sprinkle top with streusel mixture. Bake coffee cake until toothpick inserted in center comes out clean, about 40 to 45 minutes. Cool cake in pan on wire rack 1 hour to serve warm, or cool completely in pan to serve later.

EACH SERVING About 345 calories | 5 g protein | 49 g carbohydrate | 15 g total fat (4 g saturated) | 35 mg cholesterol | 260 mg sodium.

Pineapple Upside-Down Cake

We cut the pineapple slices in half to fit more fruit into the pan. Plums or apples make delicious variations (you won't need the pineapple juice).

PREP 30 minutes **BAKE** 40 minutes **MAKES** 8 servings.

2 cans (8 ounces each) pineapple slices in juice

$1/3$ cup packed brown sugar

8 tablespoons butter or margarine (1 stick), softened

1 cup cake flour (not self-rising)

1 teaspoon baking powder

$1/4$ teaspoon salt

$2/3$ cup granulated sugar

1 large egg

1 teaspoon vanilla extract

$1/3$ cup milk

1. Preheat oven to 325°F. Drain pineapple slices in sieve set over bowl. Reserve 2 tablespoons juice. Cut 8 slices pineapple in half and drain on paper towels. Refrigerate remaining slices for another use.

2. In 10-inch oven-safe skillet (if skillet is not oven-safe, wrap handle with double layer of foil), heat brown sugar and 2 tablespoons butter over medium heat until melted. Stir in reserved pineapple juice and heat to boiling; boil 1 minute. Remove skillet from heat. Decoratively arrange pineapple in skillet, overlapping slices slightly to fit.

3. In small bowl, combine flour, baking powder, and salt. In large bowl, with mixer at high speed, beat remaining 6 tablespoons butter and granulated sugar until fluffy, frequently scraping bowl with rubber spatula. Reduce speed to low; beat in egg and vanilla until well blended. Add flour mixture alternately with milk, beginning and ending with flour mixture. Beat just until blended.

4. Spoon batter over pineapple; spread evenly with rubber spatula. Bake until toothpick inserted in center of cake comes out clean, 40 to 45 minutes. Run thin knife around edges to loosen cake from side of skillet; invert onto serving plate. (If any pineapple slices stick to skillet, remove and replace on cake.) Serve warm or at room temperature.

EACH SERVING About 302 calories | 3 g protein | 46 g carbohydrate | 13 g total fat (8 g saturated) | 59 mg cholesterol | 267 mg sodium.

Plum Upside-Down Cake

Prepare as directed but substitute **1 pound plums** for pineapple. Cut plums into ¹/₂-inch-thick wedges. Heat brown sugar and 2 tablespoons butter in oven-safe skillet over medium heat until melted. Add plums and increase heat to high. Cook, stirring, until plums are glazed with brown-sugar mixture, about 1 minute.

Apple Upside-Down Cake

Prepare as directed but substitute **3 large Golden Delicious apples (1¹/₂ pounds)** for pineapple. Peel, core, and cut apples into ¹/₄-inch-thick wedges. Heat brown sugar and 2 tablespoons butter in oven-safe skillet over medium heat until melted. Add apple wedges and cook over high heat until apples are fork-tender and begin to brown, 7 to 8 minutes.

Molten Chocolate Cakes

When you cut into these warm cakes, their delectable molten centers flow out. You can assemble them up to twenty-four hours ahead and refrigerate, or you can freeze them up to two weeks. If you refrigerate the cakes, bake them for ten minutes; if they are frozen, bake for sixteen minutes. Serve with whipped cream or vanilla ice cream.

PREP 20 minutes **BAKE** 8 minutes **MAKES** 8 servings.

4 squares (4 ounces) semisweet chocolate, chopped

$^1/_2$ cup butter or margarine (1 stick), cut into pieces

$^1/_4$ cup heavy or whipping cream

$^1/_2$ teaspoon vanilla extract

$^1/_4$ cup all-purpose flour

$^1/_4$ cup granulated sugar

2 large eggs

2 large egg yolks

confectioners' sugar

whipped cream or vanilla ice cream (optional)

1. Preheat oven to 400°F. Grease eight 6-ounce custard cups. Dust with sugar.

2. In heavy 3-quart saucepan, combine chocolate, butter, and cream; heat over low heat, stirring occasionally, until butter and chocolate have melted and mixture is smooth. Remove pan from heat. Add vanilla. With wire whisk, stir in flour just until mixture is smooth.

3. In medium bowl, with mixer at high speed, beat granulated sugar, eggs, and yolks until thick and lemon-colored, about 10 minutes. Fold egg mixture, one-third at a time, into chocolate mixture until blended.

4. Divide batter evenly among prepared custard cups. Place cups in jelly-roll pan for easier handling. Bake until edges of cakes are set but centers still jiggle, 8 to 9 minutes. Cool in pan on wire rack 3 minutes. Run thin knife around edges to loosen cakes from sides of cups; invert onto dessert plates. Dust with confectioners' sugar. Serve immediately with whipped cream or ice cream, if desired.

EACH SERVING About 281 calories | 4 g protein | 20 g carbohydrate | 22 g total fat (12 g saturated) | 148 mg cholesterol | 139 mg sodium.

Apple Strudel

Layer upon layer of delicate phyllo surround a tender apple filling. Try one of the variations, too.

PREP 1 hour plus cooling **BAKE** 35 minutes **MAKES** 10 servings.

8 tablespoons butter or margarine (1 stick)

4 pounds Granny Smith apples (8 large), peeled, cored, and cut into $^1/_2$-inch pieces

$^1/_2$ cup dark seedless raisins

$^2/_3$ plus $^1/_4$ cup granulated sugar

$^1/_4$ cup walnuts, toasted and ground

$^1/_4$ cup plain dried bread crumbs

$^1/_2$ teaspoon ground cinnamon

$^1/_4$ teaspoon ground nutmeg

8 sheets (16" by 12" each) fresh or frozen (thawed) phyllo

confectioners' sugar

1. Prepare filling: In 12-inch skillet, melt 2 tablespoons butter over medium heat. Add apples, raisins, and $^2/_3$ cup granulated sugar. Cook, stirring occasionally, 15 minutes. Increase heat to medium-high and cook until liquid has evaporated and apples are soft and golden, about 15 minutes longer. Remove from heat; let filling cool completely.

2. Meanwhile, in small bowl, stir ground walnuts, bread crumbs, remaining $^1/_4$ cup granulated sugar, cinnamon, and nutmeg until thoroughly combined.

3. Preheat oven to 400°F. In 1-quart saucepan, melt remaining 6 tablespoons butter. Cut two 24-inch lengths of waxed paper. Overlap two long sides by about 2 inches.

4. On waxed paper, place 1 phyllo sheet; lightly brush with some melted butter. Sprinkle with scant 2 tablespoons bread-crumb mixture. Repeat layering with remaining phyllo, melted butter, and crumb mixture; reserve about 1 tablespoon melted butter.

5. Spoon cooled apple filling along one long side of phyllo, leaving $^3/_4$-inch borders and covering about one-third of phyllo. Starting from filling side, roll phyllo up, jelly-roll fashion, using waxed paper to help lift roll. Place roll, seam side down, on diagonal, on ungreased large cookie sheet. Tuck ends of roll under; brush with reserved 1 tablespoon melted butter. Place two foil sheets under cookie sheet; crimp edges to form rim to catch any overflow during baking.

6. Bake strudel until phyllo is golden and filling is heated through, 35 to 40 minutes. If necessary, cover strudel loosely with foil during last 10 minutes of baking to prevent overbrowning. Cool on cookie sheet on wire rack about 20 minutes. To serve, dust with confectioners' sugar and cut into thick slices.

EACH SERVING About 338 calories | 2 g protein | 58 g carbohydrate | 13 g total fat (6 g saturated) | 25 mg cholesterol | 192 mg sodium.

Cheese Strudel

In large bowl, with mixer at medium speed, beat **1 package (8 ounces) cream cheese**, softened, **¹/₄ cup sugar**, and **1 tablespoon cornstarch** until thoroughly blended. With rubber spatula, fold in **1 cup ricotta cheese**, **1 teaspoon freshly grated lemon peel**, and **¹/₂ teaspoon vanilla extract** until well combined. Cover and refrigerate filling while preparing phyllo. Prepare and fill strudel as directed but substitute cheese filling for apple filling. Bake as directed.

EACH SERVING About 301 calories | 6g protein | 23g carbohydrate | 21g total fat (12g saturated) | 56mg cholesterol | 255mg sodium.

Dried-Fruit Strudel

In 2-quart saucepan, combine **2 cups mixed dried fruit**, cut into 1-inch pieces; **1 cup dried figs**, cut into 1-inch pieces; **2 strips (3" by 1" each) lemon peel**; **1 cinnamon stick (3 inches)**; and **1³/₄ cups water**. Heat to boiling over high heat, stirring occasionally. Reduce heat to medium; cook until all liquid has been absorbed and fruit is tender, about 20 minutes longer. Cool completely. Prepare and fill strudel as directed but substitute dried-fruit filling for apple filling. Bake as directed.

EACH SERVING About 285 calories | 3 g protein | 49 g carbohydrate | 10 g total fat (5 g saturated) | 19 mg cholesterol | 175 mg sodium.

"Baked" Apples

Cooking plump, fruit-filled apples in the microwave oven saves lots of time without sacrificing a bit of flavor—and provides a delicious, warm, low-fat dessert in the middle of winter.

PREP 10 minutes **MICROWAVE** 8 minutes **MAKES** 4 servings.

4 large Golden Delicious apples (about 8 ounces each)

¼ cup pitted prunes, chopped

2 tablespoons golden raisins

2 tablespoons brown sugar

2 teaspoons margarine or butter, softened

½ teaspoon ground cinnamon

pinch salt

1. Core apples, cutting 1¼-inch-diameter cylinder from center of each, almost but not all the way through to bottom. Place apples in 8-inch square glass baking dish or shallow 1½-quart microwave-safe casserole.

2. In small bowl, combine prunes, raisins, brown sugar, margarine, cinnamon, and salt. Fill each cored apple with equal amount of prune mixture.

3. Cook apples, covered, in microwave oven on High until tender, about 8 minutes. Spoon any juices from baking dish over apples before serving.

EACH SERVING About 185 calories | 1 g protein | 44 g carbohydrate | 3 g total fat (0 g saturated) | 0 mg cholesterol | 65 mg sodium.

Apple Brown Betty

A betty is fruit baked under a bread crumb topping. Be indulgent: Pour a little heavy cream over each serving.

PREP 35 minutes **BAKE** 50 minutes **MAKES** 8 servings.

8 slices firm white bread, torn into
¹/₂-inch pieces

¹/₂ cup butter or margarine (I stick),
melted

I teaspoon ground cinnamon

2¹/₂ pounds Granny Smith apples
(6 medium), peeled, cored, and
thinly sliced

²/₃ cup packed brown sugar

2 tablespoons fresh lemon juice

I teaspoon vanilla extract

¹/₄ teaspoon ground nutmeg

1. Preheat oven to 400°F. Grease shallow 2-quart baking dish. Place bread pieces in jelly-roll pan; bake, stirring occasionally, until very lightly toasted, 12 to 15 minutes.

2. In medium bowl, combine melted butter and ¹/₂ teaspoon cinnamon. Add toasted bread pieces, tossing gently until evenly moistened.

3. In large bowl, combine apples, brown sugar, lemon juice, vanilla, nutmeg, and remaining ¹/₂ teaspoon cinnamon; toss to coat.

4. Place ¹/₂ cup toasted bread pieces in baking dish. Cover with half of apple mixture; top with 1 cup toasted bread pieces. Place remaining apple mixture on top and sprinkle evenly with remaining bread pieces, leaving 1-inch border around edges.

5. Cover with foil and bake 40 minutes. Remove foil and bake until apples are tender and bread pieces have browned, about 10 minutes longer. Let stand 10 minutes before serving.

EACH SERVING About 319 calories | 3 g protein | 51 g carbohydrate | 13 g total fat (7 g saturated) | 31 mg cholesterol | 277 mg sodium.

Broiled Brown-Sugar Bananas

A sweet, satisfying dessert with just four basic ingredients and only two grams of fat!

PREP 5 minutes **BROIL** 5 minutes **MAKES** 4 servings.

4 ripe medium bananas (about 1½ pounds), unpeeled

2 tablespoons brown sugar

1 tablespoon lower-fat margarine (40% fat)

⅛ teaspoon ground cinnamon

1. Preheat broiler. Make a lengthwise slit in each unpeeled banana, being careful not to cut all the way through and leaving 1 inch uncut at ends.

2. In cup, with fork, blend brown sugar, margarine, and cinnamon until smooth.

3. Place bananas, cut side up, on rack in broiling pan. Spoon brown-sugar mixture into split bananas. Place pan in broiler at closest position to source of heat; broil bananas until browned, about 5 minutes. Serve bananas in skins, with spoons to scoop out fruit.

EACH SERVING About 150 calories | 1 g protein | 34 g carbohydrate | 2 g total fat (1 g saturated) | 0 mg cholesterol | 20 mg sodium.

Sugar-and-Spice Blueberry Crisp

You can put this together really fast. Try it warm, with a scoop of vanilla ice cream on top.

PREP 20 minutes plus cooling **BAKE** 35 minutes **MAKES** 8 servings.

½ **cup granulated sugar**	¾ **cup quick-cooking or old-fashioned oats**
2 **tablespoons cornstarch**	½ **cup packed light brown sugar**
3 **pints blueberries**	½ **cup cold butter or margarine (1 stick), cut into pieces**
1 **tablespoon fresh lemon juice**	¾ **teaspoon ground cinnamon**
1 **cup all-purpose flour**	

1. Preheat oven to 375°F. In large bowl, combine granulated sugar and cornstarch; stir until blended. Add blueberries and lemon juice to sugar mixture; stir to coat evenly. Spoon blueberry mixture into shallow 2-quart glass or ceramic baking dish; spread evenly.

2. In same bowl, combine flour, oats, brown sugar, butter, and cinnamon. With fingers, mix until coarse crumbs form. Crumble flour mixture over blueberry mixture.

3. Place baking dish on foil-lined cookie sheet to catch any overflow during baking. Bake crisp until top is browned and fruit is bubbly at edges, 35 to 40 minutes. Cool crisp on wire rack 1 hour to serve warm, or cool completely to serve later. Reheat if desired.

EACH SERVING About 390 calories | 5 g protein | 64 g carbohydrate | 14 g total fat (8 g saturated) | 33 mg cholesterol | 135 mg sodium.

Berries-and-Cream Shortcake

A tender cake, instead of a baking-powder biscuit, is the base for this showstopper. Assemble just before serving.

PREP 40 minutes **BAKE** 25 minutes **MAKES** 10 servings.

$^1/_2$ **cup butter or margarine (1 stick), softened**

1 cup plus 1 tablespoon sugar

1$^1/_2$ cups cake flour (not self-rising)

1$^1/_2$ teaspoons baking powder

$^1/_4$ **teaspoon salt**

$^1/_2$ **cup milk**

2 large eggs

1 teaspoon vanilla extract

1 pint blueberries

$^1/_2$ **pint strawberries, hulled and cut in half**

$^1/_2$ **pint raspberries**

$^1/_2$ **pint blackberries**

$^1/_2$ **cup seedless strawberry jam**

1 cup heavy or whipping cream

1. Preheat oven to 350°F. Grease and flour two 8-inch round cake pans.

2. In large bowl, with mixer at low speed, beat butter and 1 cup sugar just until blended. Increase speed to high; beat until light and fluffy, about 5 minutes. Reduce speed to low. Add flour, baking powder, salt, milk, eggs, and vanilla; beat, frequently scraping bowl with rubber spatula, until well mixed. Increase speed to high; beat 2 minutes.

3. Spoon batter into prepared pans. Bake until toothpick inserted in center of each layer comes out clean, 25 to 30 minutes. Cool in pans on wire racks 10 minutes. Run thin knife around edges to loosen layers from sides of pans. Invert on wire racks to cool completely.

4. Meanwhile, in large bowl, gently combine blueberries, strawberries, raspberries, blackberries, and strawberry jam.

5. In small bowl, with mixer at medium speed, beat cream with remaining 1 tablespoon sugar until stiff peaks form when beaters are lifted.

6. Place 1 cake layer on cake plate; spread with half of whipped cream and top with half of fruit mixture. Place second cake layer on fruit mixture; top with remaining whipped cream and remaining fruit.

EACH SERVING About 415 calories | 4 g protein | 56 g carbohydrate | 21 g total fat (12 g saturated) | 102 mg cholesterol | 261 mg sodium.

Rhubarb-Strawberry Cobbler

We like this filling sweet-tart. If you prefer a sweeter version, just increase the sugar in the filling to three-quarters cup. Serve warm with vanilla ice cream.

PREP 45 minutes   **BAKE** 20 minutes   **MAKES** 8 servings.

1¼ **pounds rhubarb, cut into 1-inch pieces (4 cups)**

¾ **cup plus 1 teaspoon sugar**

¼ **cup water**

1 **tablespoon cornstarch**

1 **pint strawberries, hulled and cut into quarters**

1½ **cups all-purpose flour**

1½ **teaspoons baking powder**

½ **teaspoon baking soda**

¼ **teaspoon salt**

¼ **teaspoon ground cinnamon**

⅛ **teaspoon ground nutmeg**

4 **tablespoons butter or margarine, cut into pieces**

¾ **cup plus 1 tablespoon heavy or whipping cream**

1. Prepare filling: In nonreactive 3-quart saucepan, combine rhubarb and ½ cup sugar; heat to boiling over high heat, stirring constantly. Reduce heat to medium-low and cook until rhubarb is tender, about 8 minutes.

2. In cup, blend water and cornstarch until smooth. Stir strawberries and cornstarch mixture into rhubarb mixture; cook until mixture has thickened and boils, about 2 minutes. Remove from heat and keep warm.

3. Meanwhile, preheat oven to 400°F. In large bowl, combine flour, ¼ cup sugar, baking powder, baking soda, salt, cinnamon, and nutmeg. With pastry blender or two knives used scissor-fashion, cut in butter until mixture resembles coarse crumbs. Stir in ¾ cup cream just until mixture forms soft dough that leaves side of bowl.

4. On lightly floured surface, knead dough 6 to 8 times to mix thoroughly. With floured rolling pin, roll dough ½ inch thick. With 3-inch star-shaped cookie cutter or 2½-inch round cutter, cut out as many biscuits as possible. Press dough trimmings together; cut as above to make 8 biscuits in all.

5. Reheat rhubarb filling and pour into shallow 2-quart casserole or 11" by 7" baking dish. Place biscuits on top; with pastry brush, brush with remaining 1 tablespoon cream. Sprinkle with the remaining 1 teaspoon sugar. Place baking dish on foil-lined cookie sheet to catch any overflow during baking. Bake until biscuits are golden brown and rhubarb is bubbling, about 20 minutes. Cool cobbler on wire rack about 15 minutes to serve warm.

EACH SERVING About 336 calories | 4 g protein | 47 g carbohydrate | 15 g total fat (9 g saturated) | 49 mg cholesterol | 313 mg sodium.

Lemon-Sugar Crepes

These delicate crepes are perfect for a brunch menu or a light (and do-ahead) dinner party finale.

PREP 10 minutes plus chilling   COOK about 30 minutes
MAKES 12 crepes or 6 servings.

4 large lemons

3 large eggs

1 1/2 cups whole milk

2/3 cup all-purpose flour

1/2 teaspoon salt

3 tablespoons butter or margarine, melted

3/4 cup sugar

candied lemon peel (optional)

1. From lemons, grate 1/2 teaspoon peel and squeeze 3/4 cup juice. Cover and refrigerate juice to use later.

2. In blender at medium speed, blend eggs, milk, flour, salt, lemon peel, and 2 tablespoons melted butter until batter is completely smooth.

3. Transfer batter to medium bowl; cover and refrigerate at least 1 hour or overnight. Whisk batter thoroughly before using.

4. Heat nonstick 10-inch skillet or crepe pan over medium-high heat until hot. Brush pan lightly with some remaining melted butter. Pour scant 1/4 cup batter into pan; tilt pan to evenly coat bottom completely with batter. Cook crepe until top is set and underside is lightly browned, about 1 1/2 minutes.

5. With spatula, loosen edge of crepe; turn and cook other side 30 seconds (be gentle, crepes are delicate). Slip crepe onto sheet of waxed paper. Repeat with remaining batter, brushing pan lightly with butter before cooking each crepe and stacking cooked crepes between sheets of waxed paper. If not serving crepes right away, wrap in plastic and refrigerate.

6. When ready to serve, preheat oven to 350°F. Grease 13" by 9" glass baking dish. Sprinkle each crepe with 1 tablespoon sugar and 1 tablespoon lemon juice. Fold each crepe into quarters; place in baking dish, overlap-

ping slightly. Cover dish with foil; heat crepes in oven until hot, about 12 minutes. Top with candied lemon peel, if using, and serve.

EACH SERVING About 290 calories | **7 g protein** | **40 g carbohydrate** | **12 g total fat (7 g saturated)** | **136 mg cholesterol** | **340 mg sodium.**

GH Test Kitchen Tip

Crepes can be prepared and frozen up to 2 months ahead. To freeze, stack crepes between sheets of waxed paper. Wrap stacks tightly in foil; label and freeze. To use, place wrapped, frozen crepes on cookie sheet and heat in preheated 350°F oven until heated through, about 20 minutes. To serve, follow Step 6.

Peach Cobbler

A true summer treat, bursting with the flavor of ripe peaches.

PREP 45 minutes   BAKE 45 minutes   MAKES 12 servings.

PEACH FILLING

6 pounds ripe medium peaches (16 to 18), peeled, pitted, and sliced (13 cups)

^{1}/4 cup fresh lemon juice

^{2}/3 cup granulated sugar

^{1}/2 cup packed brown sugar

^{1}/4 cup cornstarch

LEMON BISCUITS

2 cups all-purpose flour

^{1}/2 cup plus 1 teaspoon granulated sugar

2^1/2 teaspoons baking powder

^{1}/4 teaspoon salt

1 teaspoon freshly grated lemon peel

4 tablespoons cold butter or margarine, cut into pieces

^{2}/3 cup plus 1 tablespoon half-and-half or light cream

1. Prepare filling: Preheat oven to 425°F. In nonreactive 8-quart saucepot, toss peaches with lemon juice. Add granulated and brown sugars and cornstarch; toss to coat. Heat over medium heat, stirring occasionally, until bubbling; boil 1 minute. Spoon hot peach mixture into 13" by 9" baking dish. Place baking dish on foil-lined cookie sheet to catch any overflow during baking. Bake 10 minutes.

2. Meanwhile, prepare biscuits: In medium bowl, combine flour, ^{1}/2 cup granulated sugar, baking powder, salt, and lemon peel. With pastry blender or two knives used scissor-fashion, cut in butter until mixture resembles coarse crumbs. Stir in ^{2}/3 cup half-and-half just until mixture forms soft dough that leaves side of bowl.

3. Turn dough onto lightly floured surface. With lightly floured hands, pat into 10" by 6" rectangle. With floured knife, cut rectangle lengthwise in half; cut each half crosswise into 6 pieces, to make 12 rectangles in all.

4. Remove dish from oven. Arrange biscuits on top of fruit. Brush biscuits with remaining 1 tablespoon half-and-half and sprinkle with remaining 1 teaspoon granulated sugar. Bake until biscuits are golden, about 35 minutes longer. To serve warm, cool cobbler on wire rack about 1 hour.

EACH SERVING About 331 calories | 4 g protein | 69 g carbohydrate | 6 g total fat (3 g saturated) | 16 mg cholesterol | 199 mg sodium.

Rosy Peach Melba

Less is more! This combination of juicy peaches and berries in a sweet rosé syrup calls for only five basic ingredients.

PREP 15 minutes plus chilling   **COOK** about 5 minutes
MAKES about 6 cups or 8 servings.

I cup water

³/₄ cup sugar

4 ripe large peaches (about 2 pounds), peeled and cut into ¹/₂-inch wedges

¹/₂ pint raspberries

1¹/₂ cups rosé or blush wine

3 tablespoons fresh lemon juice

mint sprigs

1. In 1-quart saucepan, combine water and sugar; heat to boiling over high heat. Boil 1 minute. Pour syrup into large bowl; cool to room temperature.

2. To bowl with syrup, add peaches, raspberries, wine, and lemon juice; stir gently to combine. Cover and refrigerate at least 2 hours or overnight. To serve, garnish with mint sprigs

EACH SERVING About 150 calories | 1 g protein | 31 g carbohydrate | 0 g total fat | 0 mg cholesterol | 3 mg sodium.

Peach Shortcakes with Ginger Cream

Brown-sugar biscuits are topped with a rosy fruit filling and ginger-spiked cream.

PREP 45 minutes plus standing   BAKE 15 minutes   MAKES 10 servings.

BISCUITS

2 cups all-purpose flour

¹/₃ cup packed dark brown sugar

2¹/₂ teaspoons baking powder

³/₄ teaspoon salt

1¹/₃ cups heavy or whipping cream

FRUIT TOPPING

3 ripe plums (about ¹/₂ pound), pitted and coarsely chopped

¹/₃ cup granulated sugar

5 ripe medium peaches (about 2 pounds), peeled, pitted, and sliced

GINGER CREAM

1 cup heavy or whipping cream

3 tablespoons confectioners' sugar

3 tablespoons minced crystallized ginger

slivered crystallized ginger

1. Preheat oven to 425°F. Prepare biscuits: In large bowl, combine flour and brown sugar; stir with fork, breaking up any lumps of brown sugar. Stir in baking powder and salt. Add cream and stir with fork until soft dough forms and leaves side of bowl.

2. Turn dough onto lightly floured surface; knead 4 times to mix dough thoroughly. Pat dough into a 10" by 6" rectangle. With floured knife, cut rectangle lengthwise in half; cut each half crosswise into 5 pieces to make 10 rectangles in all. With large floured spatula, transfer the rectangles to ungreased large cookie sheet. Bake until golden, about 15 minutes. Transfer to wire rack to cool.

3. Meanwhile, prepare topping: In 1-quart saucepan, combine plums and granulated sugar; heat to boiling over medium-high heat. Reduce heat to medium-low; cover and simmer until plums soften and form a sauce, about 5 minutes. Remove cover and simmer until sauce thickens slightly, 5 minutes longer. Pour sauce into large bowl; set aside to cool slightly.

4. Add peaches to bowl with plums; stir to combine. Let stand at least 30 minutes to allow flavors to develop.

5. Prepare cream: In bowl, with mixer at medium speed, beat cream, confectioners' sugar, and minced ginger until soft peaks form when beaters are lifted.

6. To serve, split biscuits. Spoon peach mixture onto bottom halves of biscuits; top with ginger cream, then biscuit tops. Garnish each with slivered ginger.

EACH SERVING About 400 calories | 4 g protein | 50 g carbohydrate | 21 g total fat (13 g saturated) | 77 mg cholesterol | 300 mg sodium.

Brown-Sugar Pear Shortcakes

Flavored with a hint of cinnamon and lemon peel, luscious pears are delicious when served over warm biscuits.

PREP 45 minutes **BAKE** 12 minutes **MAKES** 6 servings.

1 cup all-purpose flour

3/4 cup cake flour (not self-rising)

3 tablespoons granulated sugar

2 1/2 teaspoons baking powder

1/2 teaspoon salt

9 tablespoons cold butter

2/3 cup milk

2 1/2 pounds ripe Bosc pears (about 6 medium), peeled, cored, and cut lengthwise into 3/4-inch-thick wedges

1/4 cup packed light brown sugar

1/4 cup water

1/4 teaspoon ground cinnamon

2 strips lemon peel (2 1/2" by 1/2" each)

1 cup heavy or whipping cream, whipped

1. Prepare biscuits: Preheat oven to 425°F. In large bowl, mix all-purpose flour, cake flour, granulated sugar, baking powder, and salt. With pastry blender or two knives used scissor-fashion, cut in 5 tablespoons cold butter until mixture resembles coarse crumbs. Add milk, quickly stirring just until the mixture forms a soft dough that comes together (dough will be sticky).

2. Turn dough onto floured surface; gently knead for 6 to 8 strokes to mix thoroughly. With floured hands, pat dough 1 inch thick.

3. With floured 2 1/2-inch round biscuit cutter, cut out as many biscuits as possible. With pancake turner, place biscuits, 1 inch apart, on ungreased cookie sheet. Press trimmings together; cut as above to make 6 biscuits in all. Bake until golden, 12 to 15 minutes.

4. Meanwhile, prepare pears: In nonstick 12-inch skillet, melt remaining 4 tablespoons butter over medium-high heat. Add pears and cook, uncovered, stirring carefully with rubber spatula, until browned and tender, 10 to 15 minutes. Stir in brown sugar, water, cinnamon, and lemon-peel strips; cook 1 minute. Discard lemon peel.

5. To serve, with fork, split each warm biscuit horizontally in half. Spoon pear mixture onto bottom halves of biscuits; top with whipped cream, then biscuit tops.

EACH SERVING About 580 calories | 6 g protein | 67 g carbohydrate | 34 g total fat (13 g saturated) | 58 mg cholesterol | 590 mg sodium.

Roasted Pears with Marsala

Roasting pears at high heat intensifies their flavor, and the Marsala adds a sweet nuttiness. Ruby Port is a delicious alternative to the Marsala.

PREP 25 minutes   **BAKE** 40 minutes   **MAKES** 8 servings.

I lemon

8 medium Bosc pears with stems

2 teaspoons plus ¹/₃ cup sugar

¹/₂ cup sweet Marsala wine

¹/₃ cup water

2 tablespoons butter or margarine, melted

I. Preheat oven to 450°F. From lemon, with vegetable peeler, remove peel in strips (2¹/₂" by ¹/₂" each); squeeze juice.

2. With melon baller or small knife, remove cores from pears by cutting through blossom end (bottom) of unpeeled pears (do not remove stems). With pastry brush, brush cavity of each pear with lemon juice, then sprinkle each cavity with ¹/₄ teaspoon sugar.

3. In shallow 1¹/₂- to 2-quart baking dish, combine lemon peel, wine, and water. Place remaining ¹/₃ cup sugar on sheet of waxed paper. With pastry brush, brush pears with melted butter, then roll in sugar to coat. Stand pears in baking dish. Sprinkle any remaining sugar into baking dish.

4. Bake pears, basting occasionally with syrup in dish, until tender, 40 to 45 minutes.

5. Cool slightly to serve warm, or cool completely and cover and refrigerate up to 1 day. Reheat to serve warm, if you like. To serve, spoon syrup over pears.

EACH SERVING About 201 calories | I g protein | 45 g carbohydrate | 4 g total fat (2 g saturated) | 8 mg cholesterol | 31 mg sodium.

Zinfandel-Poached Pears

Easy and fat-free, the poaching liquid is reduced to a spicy ruby red syrup.

PREP 20 minutes plus chilling   COOK 45 minutes   MAKES 8 servings.

I bottle (750 ml) red zinfandel wine
(about 3 cups)

2 cups cranberry-juice cocktail

1¼ cups sugar

I cinnamon stick (3 inches)

2 whole cloves

½ teaspoon whole black
peppercorns

8 medium Bosc pears with stems

1. In nonreactive 5-quart Dutch oven, combine wine, cranberry-juice cocktail, sugar, cinnamon, cloves, and peppercorns. Heat just to boiling over high heat, stirring occasionally, until sugar has dissolved.

2. Meanwhile, peel pears, leaving stems on. With melon baller or small knife, remove cores by cutting through blossom end (bottom).

3. Place pears in wine mixture; heat to boiling. Reduce heat; cover and simmer, turning pears occasionally, until tender but not soft, 15 to 25 minutes.

4. With slotted spoon, carefully transfer pears to platter. Strain wine mixture through sieve into bowl; pour back into Dutch oven. Heat to boiling over high heat. Cook, uncovered, until liquid has reduced to 1½ cups, 15 to 30 minutes.

5. Cover pears and syrup separately and refrigerate until well chilled, at least 6 hours. To serve, spoon syrup over pears.

EACH SERVING About 352 calories | I g protein | 76 g carbohydrate |
I g total fat (0 g saturated) | 0 mg cholesterol | 6 mg sodium.

Plum Compote with Ginger Syrup

Fresh ginger and orange add extra sparkle to summer fruits.

PREP 15 minutes plus chilling **COOK** 15 minutes **MAKES** about 5 cups or 6 servings.

¹/₂ cup white zinfandel or rosé wine

¹/₂ cup water

¹/₂ cup sugar

3 strips orange peel (3" by ³/₄" each)

3 slices unpeeled fresh ginger
   (¹/₄-inch thick each)

4 whole black peppercorns

3 ripe medium plums (about
   12 ounces), unpeeled and
   each cut into 8 wedges

3 ripe medium nectarines (about
   1 pound), unpeeled and each
   cut into 8 wedges

1. In 3-quart saucepan, combine wine, water, sugar, orange peel, ginger, and peppercorns; heat to boiling over high heat. Reduce heat to low and simmer 10 minutes.

2. Add plums to syrup and simmer 5 minutes. Transfer fruit mixture to medium bowl; stir in nectarines. Cover and refrigerate at least 4 hours or overnight, stirring occasionally. Discard the ginger and orange peel before serving.

Country Plum Cobbler

Comfort food at its best: Fresh, sugared summer plums are baked under a golden biscuit crust until bubbly.

PREP 20 minutes plus cooling **BAKE** 50 minutes **MAKES** 10 servings.

2¹/₂ pounds ripe red or purple plums (about 10 medium), each pitted and cut into quarters

1/2 cup sugar

2 tablespoons all-purpose flour

1³/₄ cups reduced-fat all-purpose baking mix

¹/₄ cup yellow cornmeal

³/₄ cup water

1. Preheat oven to 400°F. In large bowl, toss plums with sugar and flour. Spoon plum mixture into shallow 2-quart ceramic or glass baking dish. Cover loosely with foil. Bake until plums are very tender, 30 to 35 minutes.

2. Remove baking dish from oven. In medium bowl, with fork, stir baking mix, cornmeal, and water just until combined. Drop 10 heaping spoonfuls of batter randomly on top of plum mixture.

3. Bake cobbler, uncovered, until biscuits are browned and plum mixture is bubbling, 20 to 25 minutes longer. Cool slightly to serve warm, or cool completely to serve later. Reheat if desired.

EACH SERVING About 190 calories | 3 g protein | 41 g carbohydrate | 2 g total fat (0 g saturated) | 0 mg cholesterol | 230 mg sodium.

Plum Kuchen

Kuchen, **German for "cake," originated in the Old World, but its many variations are enjoyed throughout America.**

PREP 30 minutes **BAKE** 30 minutes **MAKES** 10 servings.

5 large plums or 16 prune plums

1 cup all-purpose flour

¹/₂ cup sugar

1 ¹/₂ teaspoons baking powder

¹/₄ teaspoon salt

¹/₄ cup milk

¹/₄ cup butter or margarine, softened, plus 3 tablespoons

1 large egg

¹/₄ teaspoon ground cinnamon

pinch ground nutmeg

¹/₃ cup apricot jam or currant jelly

1 tablespoon boiling water

1. Preheat oven to 400°F. Grease 12" by 8" baking dish. Cut each plum in half and remove pit. If using large plums, cut each into 8 wedges.

2. In large bowl, combine flour, ¹/₄ cup sugar, baking powder, salt, milk, ¹/₄ cup butter, and egg. With mixer at low speed, beat, frequently scraping bowl with rubber spatula, until mixture leaves side of bowl and clings to beaters.

3. Spread dough in prepared baking dish. Arrange plums, skin side up, in slightly overlapping rows.

4. In small saucepan, melt remaining 3 tablespoons butter over medium heat. Stir in remaining ¹/₄ cup sugar, cinnamon, and nutmeg; spoon over plums. Bake until plums are tender, 30 to 35 minutes.

5. In small bowl, with fork, stir jelly and boiling water until smooth; with pastry brush, brush melted jelly over hot fruit. Serve warm.

EACH SERVING About 222 calories | **3 g protein** | **34 g carbohydrate** | **9 g total fat (5 g saturated)** | **44 mg cholesterol** | **226 mg sodium.**

Peach or Nectarine Kuchen

Prepare as directed but substitute **5 medium peaches**, peeled and cut into 8 wedges, or **5 medium nectarines**, not peeled and cut into 8 wedges, for plums.

EACH SERVING About 276 calories | **3 g protein** | **43 g carbohydrate** | **11 g total fat (7 g saturated)** | **55 mg cholesterol** | **283 mg sodium.**

Fruit Salad with Vanilla-Bean Syrup

Perfect alone or with a slice of Vanilla Pound Cake (page 111).

PREP 30 minutes plus chilling   **COOK** 10 minutes   **MAKES** 12 servings.

I large lemon

I vanilla bean

³/₄ cup sugar

³/₄ cup water

3 ripe mangoes, peeled and cut into 1-inch chunks

2 pints strawberries, hulled and each cut in half or into quarters if large

I medium honeydew melon (about 3 ¹/₂ pounds), peeled and cut into 1-inch chunks

1. From 1 lemon, with vegetable peeler, remove 1-inch-wide continuous strip of peel. Squeeze ¹/₄ cup juice from lemon; set aside. With knife, cut vanilla bean lengthwise in half; scrape out seeds and reserve.

2. In 1-quart saucepan, combine lemon peel, vanilla-bean seeds and pod, sugar, and water; heat to boiling over high heat. Reduce heat to medium; cook, uncovered, until syrup is slightly thickened, about 5 minutes. Remove vanilla-bean pod and lemon peel. Pour syrup into small bowl; stir in lemon juice. Cover and refrigerate syrup until chilled, about 2 hours.

3. Place mangoes, strawberries, and honeydew melon in large bowl; toss with chilled syrup.

EACH SERVING About 120 calories | 1 g protein | 31 g carbohydrate | 0 g total fat | 0 mg cholesterol | 10 mg sodium.

Autumn Fruit Compote

Dried fruits and fresh apples are poached together for a sweet compote with just a touch of citrus and cinnamon. Serve after a rich entrée such as pork or roast goose.

PREP 20 minutes plus chilling **COOK** 25 minutes **MAKES** 8 servings.

I orange

I lemon

4 medium Golden Delicious or Jonagold apples, each peeled, cored, and cut into 16 wedges

I package (8 ounces) mixed dried fruit (with pitted prunes)

I cup dried Calimyrna figs (6 ounces)

¹/₂ cup sugar

I cinnamon stick (3 inches)

3 cups water

1. From orange and lemon, with vegetable peeler, remove peel in 1-inch-wide strips. From lemon, squeeze 2 tablespoons juice (reserve orange for another use).

2. In nonreactive 4-quart saucepan, combine apples, mixed dried fruit, figs, orange and lemon peels, lemon juice, sugar, cinnamon stick, and water; heat to boiling over high heat. Reduce heat; cover and simmer until apples are tender, 15 to 20 minutes.

3. Pour fruit mixture into bowl and refrigerate at least 4 hours to blend flavors. Serve chilled (remove orange and lemon peels before serving).

EACH SERVING About 211 calories | I g protein | 55 g carbohydrate | I g total fat (0 g saturated) | 0 mg cholesterol | 8 mg sodium.

Mint Julep Cups

Bourbon and mint lend a gentle kick to fruit salad. It's just the thing to serve at a Kentucky Derby party.

PREP 25 minutes plus chilling   MAKES 6 servings.

¹/₄ cup bourbon	1 pineapple
¹/₄ cup chopped fresh mint leaves	1 pint strawberries, hulled and
2 tablespoons sugar	thickly sliced

1. In large bowl, combine bourbon, mint, and sugar until blended.

2. Prepare pineapple as directed in Tip, page 154. After coring quarters, cut them lengthwise in half, then crosswise into thin slices. Place in bowl with bourbon mixture.

3. Add strawberries; stir to combine. Refrigerate to blend flavors, about 2 hours.

EACH SERVING About 144 calories | 1 g protein | 30 g carbohydrate | 1 g total fat (0 g saturated) | 0 mg cholesterol | 4 mg sodium.

GH Test Kitchen Tip

To peel and slice a fresh pineapple, follow these easy steps:

1   Cut off crown and stem ends with a sharp chef's knife. Hold pineapple upright and cut skin off in long pieces, slicing from top to base.

2   To remove "eyes," lay pineapple on its side. Cut in at an angle on either side of row of eyes, inserting knife into fruit about ¹/₄ inch, and lift out row. Repeat at next row.

3   Cut pineapple lengthwise into quarters, slicing straight down from crown to stem end. Hold each quarter upright and cut off tough core along center edge.

Chocolate Fondue with Fruit

A fun ending to any meal.

PREP 15 minutes **COOK** 5 minutes **MAKES** 8 servings.

6 squares (6 ounces) semisweet
  chocolate, coarsely chopped

^{1}/$_2$ cup half-and-half or light cream

^{1}/$_2$ teaspoon vanilla extract

4 small bananas, peeled and cut into
  ^{1}/$_2$-inch-thick slices

2 to 3 small pears, cored and cut
  into ^{1}/$_2$-inch-thick wedges

1 pint strawberries, hulled

^{1}/$_2$ cup finely chopped almonds,
  toasted

1. In heavy 1-quart saucepan, heat chocolate and half-and-half over low heat, stirring frequently, until chocolate has melted and mixture is smooth, about 5 minutes. Stir in vanilla; keep warm.

2. To serve, arrange bananas, pears, and strawberries on large platter. Spoon sauce into small bowl; place nuts in separate small bowl. With forks or sturdy canapé picks, have guests dip fruit into chocolate sauce, then into nuts.

EACH SERVING About 249 calories | 4 g protein | 36 g carbohydrate | 13 g total fat (5 g saturated) | 6 mg cholesterol | 10 mg sodium.

Rich Vanilla-Bean Ice Cream

Using a vanilla bean instead of vanilla extract makes this classic extra special. The yolks in the custard base make it sinfully rich.

PREP 5 minutes plus chilling and freezing **COOK** 15 minutes
MAKES about 5 cups or 10 servings.

1 vanilla bean or 1 tablespoon vanilla extract	4 large egg yolks
³/₄ cup sugar	¹/₈ teaspoon salt
3 cups half-and-half or light cream	1 cup heavy or whipping cream

1. Chop vanilla bean, if using, into ¹/₄-inch pieces. In blender, process vanilla bean and sugar until vanilla bean is very finely ground.

2. In heavy 3-quart saucepan, heat half-and-half to boiling over medium-high heat.

3. Meanwhile, in medium bowl, with wire whisk, whisk egg yolks, vanilla-sugar mixture, and salt until smooth. If using vanilla extract, add with heavy cream in Step 4. Gradually whisk half-and-half into egg-yolk mixture. Return mixture to saucepan and cook over medium heat, stirring constantly, just until mixture coats back of spoon (do not boil, or it will curdle). Remove saucepan from heat.

4. Strain custard through sieve into large bowl; add heavy cream and vanilla extract, if using. Press plastic wrap onto surface of custard to prevent skin from forming. Refrigerate until well chilled, at least 2 hours or up to overnight.

5. Freeze in ice-cream maker as manufacturer directs.

EACH SERVING About 261 calories | 4 g protein | 19 g carbohydrate | 19 g total fat (11 g saturated) | 144 mg cholesterol | 71 mg sodium.

Down-Home Peach Ice Cream

An old-fashioned treat for the whole family—sweet homemade ice cream with swirls of crushed peaches.

PREP 20 minutes plus chilling and freezing **COOK** 5 minutes
MAKES about 5½ cups or 10 servings.

1 lemon	1 cup milk
6 ripe medium peaches (about 2 pounds)	1 piece vanilla bean (about 2 inches long), split in half
¾ cup sugar	⅛ teaspoon salt
1 cup heavy or whipping cream	

1. From lemon, finely grate ¼ teaspoon peel and squeeze 1 tablespoon juice. Peel and pit peaches; reserve pits. Cut peaches into chunks.

2. In food processor with knife blade attached, combine peaches, sugar, and lemon juice; pulse just to a chunky consistency. Pour peach mixture into bowl; cover and refrigerate until well chilled.

3. Meanwhile, in 2-quart saucepan, combine cream, milk, vanilla bean, salt, lemon peel, and reserved peach pits; heat over medium-high heat just until bubbles form around edge of pan. Pour cream mixture into bowl; cover and refrigerate until well chilled, at least 2 hours.

4. Strain the cream mixture through sieve into peach mixture; stir until blended. Freeze in ice-cream maker as manufacturer directs. Serve immediately or place in freezer to harden. Use within 2 weeks.

EACH SERVING About 185 calories | 2 g protein | 25 g carbohydrate | 10 g total fat (6 g saturated) | 36 mg cholesterol | 35 mg sodium.

Raspberry Ice Cream

A luxurious dessert. Top with Raspberry Sauce (page 182) for a double dose of berry flavor.

PREP 10 minutes plus chilling and freezing   **MAKES** about 4 cups or 8 servings.

4 cups fresh (about 3 half-pints) or frozen raspberries, thawed

³/₄ cup sugar

¹/₈ teaspoon salt

1 cup heavy or whipping cream

1 cup milk

1. In blender or in food processor with knife blade attached, process raspberries until smooth. With spoon, press puree through sieve into large bowl; discard seeds.

2. With wire whisk, stir sugar and salt into raspberry puree until sugar has completely dissolved. Whisk in cream and milk. Cover and refrigerate until well chilled, about 1 hour or up to 4 hours.

3. Freeze in ice-cream maker as manufacturer directs.

EACH SERVING About 224 calories | 2 g protein | 28 g carbohydrate | 12 g total fat (7 g saturated) | 45 mg cholesterol | 63 mg sodium.

Rocky-Road Freeze

You don't need an ice-cream maker to whip up this sweet treat. If you like, spoon it into a Graham Cracker–Crumb Crust (page 80).

PREP 15 minutes plus freezing **MAKES** about 4½ cups or 12 servings.

1 can (14 ounces) sweetened
   condensed milk

½ cup chocolate-flavored syrup

2 cups heavy or whipping cream

1 cup miniature marshmallows

½ cup semisweet chocolate chips

½ cup salted peanuts, chopped

1. In small bowl, combine condensed milk and chocolate syrup until blended.

2. In large bowl, with mixer at medium speed, beat cream just until stiff peaks form when beaters are lifted. Fold chocolate mixture, marshmallows, chocolate chips, and peanuts into whipped cream just until combined. Cover bowl and freeze overnight.

3. To serve, let mixture stand about 15 minutes at room temperature for easier scooping, then scoop into dessert dishes.

EACH SERVING About 351 calories | 5 g protein | 35 g carbohydrate | 23 g total fat (13 g saturated) | 66 mg cholesterol | 95 mg sodium.

Cantaloupe Sorbet

If your ice-cream maker is large enough, the recipe can easily be doubled. This sorbet is best eaten the day it's made.

PREP 15 minutes plus chilling and freezing   COOK 8 minutes
MAKES about 3¹/₂ cups or 7 servings.

1 lemon

¹/₂ cup sugar

¹/₂ cup water

1 ripe cantaloupe (3 to 3¹/₂ pounds), rind and seeds removed and flesh chopped (4 cups)

1. From lemon, with vegetable peeler, remove 2 strips peel (3" by 1" each); squeeze 1 tablespoon juice. In 2-quart saucepan, combine lemon peel, sugar, and water; heat to boiling over high heat, stirring until sugar has dissolved. Reduce heat to medium and cook 5 minutes. Set saucepan in bowl of ice water until syrup has cooled; stir in lemon juice. Strain syrup through sieve into large bowl.

2. In blender or in food processor with knife blade attached, in batches, puree cantaloupe until smooth. Stir puree into sugar syrup. Cover and refrigerate until well chilled, 2 to 4 hours.

3. Freeze in ice-cream maker as manufacturer directs.

EACH SERVING About 88 calories | 1 g protein | 22 g carbohydrate | 0 g total fat | 0 mg cholesterol | 8 mg sodium.

**Rasperry Ice Cream (left);
Cantaloupe Sorbet (right)**

Quick Blackberry Sorbet

It takes just three ingredients (plus water) to make this cool dessert. Be sure to taste the berries first: If they are too tart, use a little more sugar.

PREP 15 minutes plus freezing   **COOK** 5 minutes
MAKES about 4 cups or 8 servings.

6 cups blackberries	**1 tablespoon fresh lemon juice**
³/₄ cup sugar	**fresh mint leaves and blackberries**
³/₄ cup water	

1. In food processor with knife blade attached, process blackberries until smooth. With spoon, press puree through sieve into medium bowl; discard seeds.

2. In 2-quart saucepan, combine sugar and water; heat to boiling over medium-high heat. Reduce heat to low; simmer, stirring until sugar has dissolved, 5 minutes. Remove saucepan from heat; stir puree and lemon juice into hot sugar syrup until blended. Pour blackberry mixture into 9-inch square metal baking pan; cover and freeze until frozen solid, at least 5 hours or overnight.

3. With knife, cut blackberry mixture into 1-inch chunks. In food processor with knife blade attached, process blackberry mixture, one-half at a time, until smooth but still frozen, stopping processor frequently to scrape down side. Serve immediately or spoon into freezer-safe container; freeze up to 1 month.

4. To serve, if too firm to scoop, let sorbet stand at room temperature to soften slightly, 10 to 15 minutes. Garnish each serving with mint leaves and blackberries.

EACH SERVING About 125 calories | 1 g protein | 32 g carbohydrate | 0 g total fat | 0 mg cholesterol | 0 mg sodium.

Pink Grapefruit Sorbet

A welcome change from the usual flavors; serve it with a splash of vodka or dark rum.

PREP 20 minutes plus cooling and freezing   COOK 15 minutes
MAKES about 5 cups or 10 servings.

3 large pink or red grapefruit

4 cups water

1 cup sugar

1/4 cup light corn syrup

drop red food coloring (optional)

1. From grapefruit, with vegetable peeler, remove 3 strips peel (4" by 3/4" each); squeeze 2 cups juice.

2. In 2-quart saucepan, combine water, sugar, corn syrup, and grapefruit peel; heat to boiling over high heat, stirring until sugar has dissolved. Reduce heat to medium and cook 2 minutes. Set saucepan in bowl of *ice water* until syrup has cooled; discard peel.

3. Strain grapefruit juice through sieve into large bowl. With spoon, press pulp to extract juice; discard pulp. Stir in sugar syrup and food coloring, if using. Pour into 9-inch square metal baking pan; cover and freeze, stirring occasionally, until partially frozen, about 4 hours.

4. In food processor with knife blade attached, process sorbet until smooth but still frozen, stopping processor frequently to scrape down side. Return to pan; cover and freeze until almost firm, 3 to 4 hours.

5. To serve, process sorbet in food processor until smooth.

EACH SERVING About 120 calories | 0 g protein | 31 g carbohydrate |
0 g total fat | 0 mg cholesterol | 11 mg sodium.

Strawberry Granita

Make this granita with flavorful ripe strawberries for the quintessential early-summer dessert.

PREP 10 minutes plus cooling and freezing COOK 8 minutes
MAKES about 6 cups or 12 servings.

1 cup water	2 pints strawberries, hulled
¹/₂ cup sugar	1 tablespoon fresh lemon juice

1. In 2-quart saucepan, combine water and sugar; heat to boiling over high heat, stirring until sugar has dissolved. Reduce heat to medium and cook 5 minutes. Set saucepan in bowl of ice water until syrup has cooled.

2. Meanwhile, in blender or in food processor with knife blade attached, process strawberries until smooth. Stir strawberry puree and lemon juice into sugar syrup; pour into 9-inch square metal baking pan. Cover and freeze until partially frozen, about 2 hours.

3. Stir granita with a fork to break up chunks.

EACH SERVING About 49 calories | 0 g protein | 12 g carbohydrate |
0 g total fat | 0 mg cholesterol | 1 mg sodium.

Lemon Ice in Lemon Cups

Serve these at your next dinner party with a sprightly sprig of fresh mint on each.

PREP 30 minutes plus freezing   **COOK** 5 minutes   **MAKES** 6 servings.

6 large lemons	**I envelope unflavored gelatin**
I cup sugar	**2$^1/_4$ cups water**

1. Cut off top one-third of each lemon. Grate peel from lemon tops. Wrap 1 teaspoon grated peel in plastic wrap for garnish and refrigerate; reserve remaining grated peel. Squeeze $^3/_4$ cup juice from lemons. With melon baller, remove all pulp and membrane; discard. Cut thin slice off bottom of each lemon cup so it sits flat. Place lemon cups in plastic bag and freeze until ready to fill.

2. In 2-quart saucepan, combine sugar and gelatin; stir in water. Let stand 2 minutes to soften gelatin slightly. Cook over medium-low heat, stirring constantly, until gelatin has completely dissolved. Remove saucepan from heat. Stir in lemon juice and reserved grated peel.

3. Pour lemon mixture into 9-inch square metal baking pan. Cover and freeze, stirring occasionally, until partially frozen, about 2 hours. Place large bowl in refrigerator to chill.

4. Spoon lemon mixture into chilled bowl. With mixer at medium speed, beat until smooth but still frozen. Return mixture to pan; cover and freeze until partially frozen, about 2 hours. Return bowl to refrigerator.

5. Spoon lemon mixture into chilled bowl and beat until smooth but still frozen. Cover and freeze until firm, about 3 hours.

6. Spoon lemon ice into frozen lemon cups. Sprinkle with remaining 1 teaspoon grated lemon peel. Serve immediately, or freeze up to 2 hours.

EACH SERVING About 141 calories | I g protein | 36 g carbohydrate | 0 g total fat | 0 mg cholesterol | 3 mg sodium.

Sorbet-and-Cream Cake

Here's a colorful dessert for a festive meal. If you prefer, substitute raspberry and passion fruit sorbets (or your favorite flavors) for the strawberry and mango.

PREP 30 minutes plus freezing BAKE 10 minutes MAKES 20 servings.

I cup vanilla wafer crumbs
   (30 cookies)

4 tablespoons butter or margarine,
   melted

1/2 teaspoon freshly grated lime peel

2 pints vanilla ice cream

I pint strawberry sorbet

I pint mango sorbet

I pint lemon sorbet

I ripe mango, peeled and sliced

fresh raspberries

1. Preheat oven to 375°F. In 9" by 3" springform pan, with fork, stir wafer crumbs, melted butter, and lime peel until crumbs are evenly moistened. With hands, press mixture firmly onto bottom of pan. Bake crust 10 minutes. Freeze until well chilled, about 30 minutes.

2. Meanwhile, place 1 pint vanilla ice cream and strawberry, mango, and lemon sorbets in refrigerator to soften slightly, about 30 minutes.

3. Arrange alternating scoops of vanilla ice cream and strawberry, mango, and lemon sorbets over crust in two layers; with rubber spatula, press down to eliminate air pockets. Freeze until ice cream is firm, about 30 minutes.

4. Meanwhile, place remaining 1 pint vanilla ice cream in refrigerator to soften slightly. With narrow metal spatula, evenly spread vanilla ice cream over ice-cream layers. Cover and freeze until firm, at least 4 hours or up to 1 day.

5. To serve, dip small knife in hot water, shaking off excess; run knife around edge of pan to loosen cake from pan. Remove side of pan; place cake on platter. Let stand about 15 minutes at room temperature for easier slicing. Arrange mango slices and raspberries decoratively on top of cake.

EACH SERVING About 161 calories | 1 g protein | 27 g carbohydrate |
6 g total fat (3 g saturated) | 18 mg cholesterol | 63 mg sodium.

Banana-Caramel Tart

Dulce de leche is a sweet Latin dessert made by slowly cooking down milk (usually sweetened, condensed) until it's thick and almost caramelized. Traditionally, it's spread on bread or crackers or used in pastries and cakes. But now you can get the *dulce de leche* flavor in luscious ice cream, which we layered with fresh bananas over a no-bake pecan cookie crust.

PREP 30 minutes plus freezing **MAKES** 12 servings.

SHORTBREAD COOKIE CRUST

18 pecan shortbread cookies (about 14 ounces)

1 cup pecans, toasted

2 tablespoons butter or margarine, melted

ICE-CREAM FILLING

2 pints dulce de leche ice cream, softened

4 ripe, medium bananas

1. Prepare crust: In food processor with knife blade attached, process cookies and $1/2$ cup pecans until very finely ground. With food processor running, drizzle in butter until blended.

2. With hands, press cookie mixture evenly onto bottom and up side of 11" by 1" round tart pan with removable bottom. Freeze until crust is firm, about 15 minutes. Meanwhile, coarsely chop remaining $1/2$ cup pecans; set aside.

3. Prepare filling: Spread 1 pint ice cream evenly over crust. Cut 3 bananas crosswise into $1/4$-inch-thick slices and arrange them in single layer over ice cream. Cover tart with plastic wrap and freeze 30 minutes.

4. Spread remaining pint ice cream over banana layer. Slice remaining banana. Arrange banana slices, overlapping slightly, on ice cream in a ring 2 inches from edge of tart pan. Sprinkle top of tart with chopped pecans. Cover and freeze until firm, at least 6 hours. If not serving tart same day, wrap and freeze up to 2 weeks.

5. To serve, uncover tart and let stand at room temperature 10 minutes to soften slightly for easier slicing. Remove side of pan and place tart on platter.

EACH SERVING About 490 calories | 6 g protein | 47 g carbohydrate | 31 g total fat (12 g saturated) | 75 mg cholesterol | 200 mg sodium.

Frozen Key Lime Pie

Quick, cool, and refreshing—what could be better during the heat of summer?

PREP 20 minutes plus cooling and freezing BAKE 10 minutes MAKES 10 servings.

Graham Cracker–Crumb Crust
  (page 80)

4 limes

1 can (14 ounces) sweetened
  condensed milk

1 cup heavy or whipping cream

1. Prepare Graham Cracker–Crumb Crust as directed. Cool completely.

2. From limes, grate 1 tablespoon peel and squeeze 1/2 cup juice. In large bowl, with wire whisk, stir condensed milk and lime peel and juice until well blended.

3. In medium bowl, with mixer at medium speed, beat cream until stiff peaks form when beaters are lifted. Fold whipped cream, one-third at a time, into lime mixture just until blended.

4. Pour mixture into cooled crust. Cover and freeze at least 3 hours or up to 1 month. Let pie stand 10 minutes at room temperature for easier slicing.

EACH SERVING About 319 calories | 5 g protein | 36 g carbohydrate |
18 g total fat (11 g saturated) | 59 mg cholesterol | 196 mg sodium.

Frozen Strawberry Margarita Pie

If you love margaritas, you'll love this; the delectable filling is made with whipped cream and fresh lime juice.

PREP 25 minutes plus cooling and freezing BAKE 10 minutes MAKES 10 servings.

CRUMB CRUST

1 1/2 cups vanilla wafer crumbs

5 tablespoons margarine or butter, melted

1/2 teaspoon freshly grated lime peel

STRAWBERRY FILLING

1 pint strawverries

2 limes

3/4 cup sugar

1 can (14 ounces) sweetened condensed milk

2 tablespoons orange-flavored liqueur

1 cup heavy or whipping cream

1. Prepare crust: Preheat oven to 375°F. In 9-inch pie plate, with fork, stir wafer crumbs, melted margarine, and lime peel until crumbs are evenly moistened. With hand, press mixture onto bottom and up side of pie plate, making a small rim. Bake 10 minutes. Cool crust in pie plate on wire rack.

2. Prepare filling: Hull 2 cups strawberries; reserve remaining berries for garnish. From limes, grate 1 teaspoon peel and squeeze 1/4 cup juice. In food processor with knife blade attached, pulse hulled berries, lime peel and juice, condensed milk, and liqueur until almost smooth. Transfer mixture to large bowl.

3. In small bowl, with mixer at medium speed, beat 2/3 cup cream until stiff peaks form when beaters are lifted; reserve remaining unwhipped cream for garnish. Gently fold whipped cream, one-third at a time, into strawberry mixture.

4. Pour filling into cooled crust. Freeze until almost firm, at least 4 hours. (If not serving pie on same day, wrap frozen pie in foil or plastic wrap and freeze up to 1 week.)

5. If pie is frozen completely, let stand at room temperature 10 minutes before serving for easier slicing. Cut each reserved strawberry in half. In small bowl, with mixer at medium speed, beat remaining $^1/_3$ cup cream just until stiff peaks form when beaters are lifted. Mound whipped cream in center of pie and top with strawberry halves.

EACH SERVING About 360 calories | 5 g protein | 39 g carbohydrate | 21 g total fat (9 g saturated) | 57 mg cholesterol | 180 mg sodium.

Holiday Baked Alaska with Red-Raspberry Sauce

A new take on an old favorite, featuring ladyfingers, vanilla ice cream, and ruby-red sorbet covered with a dome of meringue. Do-ahead: Make and freeze the cake without meringue up to two weeks before serving. The sauce can be made up to three days ahead. The baked meringue-topped cake can be frozen up to four hours before serving. Just remember to remove it from the freezer twenty minutes before serving for easier slicing.

PREP I hour 30 minutes plus freezing **BAKE** 2 minutes **MAKES** I6 servings.

ICE-CREAM CAKE

2 pints vanilla ice cream

3 packages (3 to 4^1/$_2$ ounces each) sponge-type ladyfingers

2 pints raspberry sorbet

RED-RASPBERRY SAUCE

I package (10 ounces) frozen raspberries in quick-thaw pouch, thawed

2 tablespoons seedless raspberry jam

I tablespoon orange-flavored liqueur

MERINGUE

4 large egg whites

^{3}/$_4$ cup sugar

4 teaspoons water

^{1}/$_4$ teaspoon salt

^{1}/$_4$ teaspoon cream of tartar

1. Prepare ice-cream cake: Place vanilla ice cream in large bowl; let stand at room temperature to soften slightly, stirring occasionally, until spreadable.

2. Meanwhile, split each ladyfinger in half lengthwise. Line bottom and side of 10" by 1^1/$_2$" round baking dish, shallow 1^1/$_2$-quart round casserole, or 9^1/$_2$-inch deep-dish pie plate with about two-thirds of ladyfingers, placing ladyfingers, rounded side out, around side and allowing ladyfingers to extend above rim of baking dish.

3. Spoon vanilla ice cream into lined dish. Smooth with small metal spatula; freeze until ice cream is firm, 30 minutes.

4. Place raspberry sorbet in large bowl; let stand at room temperature to soften slightly, stirring occasionally, until spreadable. Spoon raspberry sorbet on top of ice cream, smoothing with spatula. Top sorbet with remaining ladyfingers, rounded side up. Cover cake with waxed paper and foil; freeze until firm, at least 6 hours.

5. Prepare sauce: In food processor with knife blade attached, process raspberries, jam, and liqueur until smooth. Pour sauce into small pitcher to serve. Cover and refrigerate until ready to use.

6. About 30 minutes before serving, prepare meringue: Preheat oven to 500°F. In large bowl set over simmering water or in top of double boiler, with handheld mixer at medium speed, beat egg whites, sugar, water, salt, and cream of tartar until soft peaks form when beaters are lifted and temperature on thermometer reaches 160°F, 12 to 14 minutes. Transfer bowl with meringue to work surface. Beat meringue until stiff peaks form when beaters are lifted, 8 to 10 minutes longer.

7. Remove cake from freezer. Spoon meringue over top of cake, sealing meringue to edge and swirling with spoon to make attractive top. Bake until meringue is lightly browned, 2 to 3 minutes. Place on heat-safe platter. Serve immediately with red-raspberry sauce or freeze for up to 4 hours. Remove from freezer 20 minutes before serving.

EACH SERVING About 250 calories | 4 g protein | 40 g carbohydrate |
5 g total fat (3 g saturated) | 73 mg cholesterol | 95 mg sodium.

Sugar-and-Spice Ice-Cream Sandwiches

Cookies spiced up with cinnamon, ginger, and a hint of pepper make the perfect match for homemade (or store-bought) ice cream. Try peach (page 157) or raspberry (page 158) for a special treat.

PREP 10 minutes plus freezing **BAKE** 10 to 12 minutes per batch
MAKES 16 sandwiches.

1 1/2 cups all-purpose flour

1/2 cup unsweetened cocoa

2 teaspoons ground ginger

1 teaspoon ground cinnamon

1 teaspoon baking powder

1/2 teaspoon baking soda

1/2 teaspoon salt

1/2 teaspoon finely ground black pepper

1 cup packed dark brown sugar

1/2 cup margarine or butter (1 stick), softened

1 large egg

1 teaspoon vanilla extract

1 pint strawberry ice cream, softened

1. In medium bowl, combine flour, cocoa, ginger, cinnamon, baking powder, baking soda, salt, and pepper.

2. In large bowl, with mixer at medium speed, beat brown sugar and margarine until creamy. Reduce speed to low. Add egg and vanilla; beat until well blended. Add flour mixture; beat just until blended.

3. Divide dough into 4 equal pieces. Shape each piece into 3" by 2" rectangular block 1 1/2 inches high. Wrap each block with waxed paper or plastic wrap and freeze until very firm, at least 1 hour or up to overnight.

4. Preheat oven to 350°F. Slice 1 cookie-dough block lengthwise into 8 equal slices. Place slices, about 1 inch apart, on large ungreased cookie sheet. Repeat with another block of dough. (Work quickly with dough to prevent cookies from becoming misshapen as the dough softens.)

5. Bake cookies 10 to 12 minutes. Cool completely on cookie sheet on wire rack. Transfer cookies to plate. Repeat with remaining dough.

6. To make sandwiches, place 16 cookies on 15½″ by 10½″ jelly-roll pan. Place about 1 heaping tablespoon softened ice cream on top of each cookie. With small metal spatula, spread ice cream on each cookie, almost to edges. Top with remaining cookies to make 16 sandwiches in all. Wrap individually in foil and freeze at least 1 hour or up to 1 week.

EACH SANDWICH About 200 calories | 3 g protein | 30 g carbohydrate | 9 g total fat (3 g saturated) | 29 mg cholesterol | 240 mg sodium.

Tulipes

For an elegant ending to a dinner party or other occasion, serve your favorite ice cream in these delicate cookie shells (see photo on page 155).

PREP 30 minutes **BAKE** 5 minutes per batch **MAKES** about 12 tulipes.

3 large egg whites

³/₄ cup confectioners' sugar

¹/₂ cup all-purpose flour

6 tablespoons butter, melted (do not use margarine)

¹/₂ teaspoon vanilla extract

¹/₄ teaspoon salt

I quart ice cream or sorbet

1. Preheat oven to 350°F. Grease large cookie sheet.

2. In large bowl, with wire whisk, beat egg whites, confectioners' sugar, and flour until well blended. Beat in melted butter, vanilla, and salt.

3. Make 2 cookies by dropping batter by heaping tablespoons, 4 inches apart, on prepared cookie sheet. With narrow metal spatula, spread batter to form 4-inch rounds. Bake cookies until golden around edges, 5 to 7 minutes.

4. Place two 2-inch-diameter glasses upside down on surface. With spatula quickly lift 1 hot cookie and gently shape over bottom of glass. Shape second cookie. When cookies are cool, transfer to wire rack. (If cookies become too firm to shape, return them to cookie sheet and place in oven to soften slightly.)

5. Repeat Steps 3 and 4 with remaining batter. (Batter will become slightly thicker upon standing.) Store tulipes in single layer in airtight container at room temperature. To serve, place on dessert plates and fill with ice cream.

EACH SERVING WITH ICE CREAM About 192 calories | 3 g protein | 22 g carbohydrate | 11 g total fat (7 g saturated) | 35 mg cholesterol | 155 mg sodium.

Finishing Touches

Hot Fudge Sauce

Hot Fudge Sauce

Use this rich chocolaty sauce as a topping for ice cream or other desserts. Unsweetened cocoa powder makes it easy to prepare.

PREP 5 minutes   **COOK** 5 minutes   **MAKES** about 1¼ cups.

¾ cup sugar

½ cup unsweetened cocoa

½ cup heavy or whipping cream

4 tablespoons butter or margarine, cut into pieces

1 teaspoon vanilla extract

In heavy 1-quart saucepan, combine sugar, cocoa, cream, and butter; heat to boiling over high heat, stirring frequently. Remove saucepan from heat; stir in vanilla. Serve warm, or cool completely, then cover and refrigerate up to 2 weeks. Gently reheat before using.

EACH TABLESPOON About 75 calories | 1 g protein | 9 g carbohydrate | 5 g total fat (3 g saturated) | 14 mg cholesterol | 26 mg sodium.

Butterscotch Sauce

An old-fashioned favorite—divine in an ice-cream sundae but also wonderful with apple pie.

PREP 5 minutes   **COOK** 5 minutes   **MAKES** 1⅓ cups.

I cup packed brown sugar

½ cup heavy or whipping cream

⅓ cup light corn syrup

2 tablespoons butter or margarine

I teaspoon distilled white vinegar

⅛ teaspoon salt

I teaspoon vanilla extract

In heavy 3-quart saucepan, combine brown sugar, cream, corn syrup, butter, vinegar, and salt; heat to boiling over high heat, stirring occasionally. Reduce heat and simmer 2 minutes. Remove saucepan from heat; stir in vanilla. Serve warm, or cover and refrigerate up to 1 week.

EACH TABLESPOON About 84 calories | 0 g protein | 14 g carbohydrate | 3 g total fat (2 g saturated) | 11 mg cholesterol | 38 mg sodium.

Raspberry Sauce

Bright in color and tart in flavor, this red sauce dresses up cakes from Chocolate Truffle (page 82) to Angel Food (page 104), as well as tarts, puddings, ice cream, or fresh fruit.

PREP 5 minutes   **COOK** 5 minutes   **MAKES** 1 cup.

1 package (10 ounces) frozen
   raspberries in syrup, thawed

2 tablespoons red currant jelly

2 teaspoons cornstarch

1. With back of spoon, press raspberries through fine sieve into nonreactive 2-quart saucepan; discard seeds. Stir in jelly and cornstarch. Heat to boiling over high heat, stirring constantly; boil 1 minute.

2. Serve at room temperature, or cover and refrigerate up to 2 days.

EACH TABLESPOON About 26 calories | 0 g protein | 7 g carbohydrate | 0 g total fat | 0 mg cholesterol | 1 mg sodium.

Sweetened Whipped Cream

Feel free to flavor the cream with vanilla or with one of the other tasty suggestions.

PREP 10 minutes   **MAKES** about 2 cups.

1 cup heavy or whipping cream
   (preferably not ultrapasteurized),
   well chilled

1 to 2 tablespoons sugar

1 teaspoon vanilla extract;
   1/8 teaspoon almond extract;
   or 1 tablespoon brandy, rum,
   or orange-flavored liqueur

1. Chill medium bowl and beaters 20 minutes.

2. In chilled bowl, with mixer at medium speed, beat cream, sugar, and vanilla until soft peaks form when beaters are lifted. Do not overbeat or cream will separate.

EACH TABLESPOON About 28 calories | 0 g protein | 1 g carbohydrate | 3 g total fat (2 g saturated) | 10 mg cholesterol | 3 mg sodium.

Pralines

This is the classic pecan candy from the South. Use dark brown sugar if you prefer a richer flavor.

PREP 15 minutes **COOK** 25 minutes **MAKES** about 40 pralines.

½ cup butter (1 stick), cut into pieces (do not use margarine)

2 cups granulated sugar

1 cup packed light brown sugar

1 cup heavy or whipping cream

2 tablespoons light corn syrup

2 cups pecans (8 ounces), toasted and coarsely chopped

1 teaspoon vanilla extract

1. Grease 2 or 3 cookie sheets.

2. In heavy 3-quart saucepan, combine butter, granulated and brown sugars, cream, and corn syrup; cook over medium heat, stirring occasionally, until sugars have dissolved and syrup is bubbling.

3. Set candy thermometer in place and continue cooking, without stirring, until temperature reaches 230° to 234°F or thread stage (when small amount of syrup forms a fine thin thread in the air as it falls from the spoon), about 8 minutes.

4. Add pecans and vanilla; stir until bubbling subsides. Heat to boiling. Continue cooking until candy temperature reaches 244° to 248°F or firm-ball stage (when small amount of syrup forms a firm ball after standing in very cold water for about 30 seconds).

5. Remove saucepan from heat and stir vigorously until syrup has thickened and turns opaque, about 3 minutes.

6. Working quickly, drop mixture by tablespoons, at least 1 inch apart, on prepared cookie sheets (stir briefly over low heat if mixture gets too thick). Cool pralines completely. Store with waxed paper between layers in airtight container at room temperature up to 1 week, or freeze up to 3 months.

EACH PRALINE About 144 calories | 1 g protein | 17 g carbohydrate | 9 g total fat (3 g saturated) | 14 mg cholesterol | 29 mg sodium.

Chocolate and Hazelnut Truffles

Use the best chocolate to give these truffles European flair. If you wish, add two tablespoons of coffee-, orange-, or almond-flavored liqueur to the melted-chocolate mixture.

PREP 25 minutes plus chilling **MAKES** 32 truffles.

8 squares (8 ounces) bittersweet chocolate or 6 squares (6 ounces) semisweet chocolate plus 2 squares (2 ounces) unsweetened chocolate, coarsely chopped

$^1/_2$ cup heavy or whipping cream

3 tablespoons butter, cut into pieces and softened (do not use margarine)

$^1/_3$ cup hazelnuts (filberts), toasted and skinned (see page 109), finely chopped

3 tablespoons unsweetened cocoa

1. Line $8^1/_2$" by $4^1/_2$" loaf pan with plastic wrap; smooth out wrinkles. In food processor with knife blade attached, process chocolate until finely ground.

2. In 1-quart saucepan, heat cream to simmering over medium-high heat. Add to chocolate in food processor and puree until smooth. Add butter and process until smooth.

3. Pour chocolate mixture into prepared pan; spread evenly. Refrigerate until cool and firm enough to handle, about 3 hours.

4. Remove chocolate mixture from pan by lifting edges of plastic wrap. Invert chocolate block onto cutting board; discard plastic wrap. Cut chocolate lengthwise into 4 strips, then cut each strip crosswise into 8 pieces. (To cut chocolate easily, dip knife in hot water and wipe dry; repeat as needed.) With cool hands, quickly roll each square into ball. Roll 16 truffles in chopped hazelnuts and remaining 16 truffles in cocoa. Store in single layer in waxed paper–lined airtight container. Refrigerate up to 1 week, or freeze up to 1 month. Remove from freezer 5 minutes before serving.

EACH TRUFFLE About 66 calories | 1 g protein | 5 g carbohydrate | 6 g total fat (3 g saturated) | 8 mg cholesterol | 13 mg sodium.

Mocha Truffles

Make these truffles up to two weeks ahead—they're perfect for holiday gift giving.

PREP 30 minutes plus chilling   COOK about 5 minutes
MAKES about 4 dozen truffles.

12 squares (12 ounces) semisweet chocolate, coarsely chopped

¾ cup sweetened condensed milk

1 tablespoon instant-coffee powder or granules

2 tablespoons coffee-flavored liqueur

⅛ teaspoon salt

unsweetened cocoa

1. In heavy 2-quart saucepan, melt chocolate over low heat, stirring occasionally. Stir in condensed milk, instant-coffee powder, liqueur, and salt until well mixed. Refrigerate mixture until easy to shape, about 30 minutes.

2. Place cocoa in small bowl. Dust hands with cocoa, then shape 1 rounded teaspoon chocolate mixture into a ball. Dip ball in cocoa. Repeat with remaining chocolate mixture. Store with waxed paper between layers in tightly covered container. Refrigerate up to 2 weeks.

EACH TRUFFLE About 55 calories | 1 g protein | 7 g carbohydrate | 3 g total fat (2 g saturated) | 2 mg cholesterol | 10 mg sodium.

Chocolate Leaves

Use only nontoxic, pesticide-free leaves, available at florist shops. Lemon, gardenia, grape, magnolia, nasturtium, rose, and violet are good choices.

PREP 30 minutes plus chilling **MAKES** 12 leaves.

12 lemon leaves

1 package (6 ounces) semisweet chocolate chips

¹/₄ cup vegetable shortening

1. Wash leaves in warm soapy water; pat thoroughly dry with paper towels.

2. In heavy 1-quart saucepan, combine chocolate chips and shortening; heat over low heat, stirring frequently, until melted and smooth.

3. With pastry brush or small metal spatula, spread layer of melted chocolate mixture on underside (back) of each leaf (underside will give more distinct leaf design). Place chocolate-coated leaves, chocolate side up, on waxed paper–lined cookie sheet. Refrigerate until chocolate is firm, about 30 minutes.

4. With cool hands, carefully and gently peel each leaf away from chocolate.

Chocolate Curls

Use these curls to garnish ice cream, cakes, and pies.

PREP 15 minutes plus chilling

1 package (6 ounces) semisweet chocolate chips

2 tablespoons vegetable shortening

1. Line a 5³/₄" by 3¹/₄" loaf pan with foil. In heavy 1-quart saucepan, combine chocolate chips and shortening; heat over low heat, stirring frequently, until melted and smooth.

2. Pour chocolate mixture into prepared pan. Refrigerate until chocolate is set, about 2 hours.

3. Remove chocolate from pan by lifting edges of foil. Using vegetable peeler and working over waxed paper, draw blade across surface of chocolate to make large curls. If chocolate is too cold and curls break, let chocolate stand at room temperature until slightly softened, about 30 minutes. Use toothpick or wooden skewer to transfer for garnish.

Index

Photography Credits